Letters to a Young Academic

Seeking Teachable Moments

Guy Randall McPherson

Rowman & Littlefield Education
Lanham, Maryland • Toronto • Oxford
2006

Published in the United States of America
by Rowman & Littlefield Education
A Division of Rowman & Littlefield Publishers, Inc.
A wholly owned subsidiary of The Rowman &
Littlefield Publishing Group, Inc.
4501 Forbes Boulevard, Suite 200, Lanham, Maryland
20706
www.rowmaneducation.com

PO Box 317
Oxford
OX2 9RU, UK

Copyright © 2006 by Guy R. McPherson

All rights reserved. No part of this publication may be reproduced, stored in a retrieval system, or transmitted in any form or by any means, electronic, mechanical, photocopying, recording, or otherwise, without the prior permission of the publisher.

British Library Cataloguing in Publication Information Available

Library of Congress Cataloging-in-Publication Data

McPherson, Guy R. (Guy Randall), 1960-
  Letters to a young academic : seeking teachable moments / Guy Randall McPherson.
      p. cm.
  Includes index.
  ISBN-13: 978-1-57886-337-6 (hardcover : alk. paper)
  ISBN-10: 1-57886-337-6 (hardcover : alk. paper)
  ISBN-13: 978-1-57886-338-4 (pbk. : alk. paper)
  ISBN-10: 1-57886-338-4 (pbk. : alk. paper)
  1. College teaching—United States. 2. College teachers—United States. 3. Effective teaching—United States. I. Title.
  LB2331.M397 2006
  378.1'2—dc22

2005026773

I started writing these letters to Jake Weltzin.

I ended up writing to Sara Jensen, Erika Geiger, David Hall, Chris McDonald, Theresa Mau-Crimmins, Dana Backer, Heather Schussman, Cindy Salo, Jose Villanueva-Diaz, Margi Brooks, Cody Wienk, Margaret Evans, Juliann Aukema, Roxane Johnson, Heather Germaine, Laurie Abbott, Andy Hubbard, Svenje Mehlert, Sam Drake, Kathryn Haworth, Charles Nyandiga, Jim McPherson, Graeme Cumming, David Merritt, Kristina Rothley, Jake Vander Zanden, Jeff Su, Bob Hilderbrand, and Peter Jacobson.

The family of David H. Smith had a lot to do with it.

Contents

Acknowledgments	vii
Introduction	ix
Chapter I	1
Chapter II	15
Chapter III	27
Chapter IV	41
Chapter V	49
Chapter VI	57
Chapter VII	67
Chapter VIII	73
Chapter IX	79
Chapter X	85
Chapter XI	97
Chapter XII	105
Chapter XIII	111
Chapter XIV	125
Chapter XV	127
Chapter XVI	133
Chapter XVII	145

Chapter XVIII	149
Chapter XIX	151
Chapter XX	157
About the Author	163

Acknowledgments

Dozens of students and postdoctoral researchers inspired these letters and enriched my life. Most of them are mentioned in the book's dedication, and I apologize now for those I have no doubt forgotten. Most of the letters were composed at The Nature Conservancy's Lichty Ecological Research Center near Cliff, New Mexico, and subsequently reviewed and improved by Sara Jensen, Sheila Merrigan, Carol Wallace, Chris McDonald, and Jim McPherson. Peter Russell facilitated my sabbatical leave at the Lichty Center and made my stay there pleasant and productive. Considerable patience, guidance, insight, and love came from my exemplary first teachers, Jim and Edna McPherson.

As always, thanks to Sheila Merrigan for everything.

Introduction

The following pages are my latest attempt to provide advice to aspiring and early-career academicians. The endeavor is simultaneously humble and arrogant; the former because I am not particularly qualified to provide the advice, the latter because nobody else is, either, and because the advice was not specifically solicited. I write "specifically" because I have provided most of the advice in these letters in various forms during the last two decades, albeit never in a single compilation such as this. (Full disclosure: Not much of the advice was solicited when I gave it the first time, either.)

Academicians have much to read, and advice for them abounds. Furthermore, early-career members of the academy are burdened with countless other responsibilities. Why read this particular book? I offer two reasons for spending precious time with me on this journey. First, this collection of letters is written in a more personal voice than most other published works; as such, I hope you will feel as if the letters are written specifically to you. Second, its intentional brevity suggests that an investment of a few hours will reward the typical reader with a many-fold return.

The enclosed letters were inspired by Rainer Maria Rilke's *Letters to a Young Poet* and more recently by Christopher Hitchens' *Letters to a Young Contrarian.* They are intended to inspire, or at least amuse, academicians in all fields, and they are written to all of my former students as if they were one person.

I

Your idealism is so refreshing it borders on infectious. It threatens to dent my cynicism about intellectual life, tainted as it is by politics. My enthusiasm has been rekindled by your optimism, thereby inspiring me to pursue this advice-filled correspondence. Your idealism about inquisitive young students, wise and tolerant professors, and cooperative colleagues seems so pure that I am compelled to warn you about the trouble ahead. I seem old, jaded, and generally burned out in comparison to you, though I've not previously thought of myself in these terms. I apologize if the warning is coming too late, if you have already been afflicted.

If a career in the academy torments you from afar (or even from very near), if you feel a relentless call to the life of the mind, if you cannot walk away from long days for little pay because you are bound by an unspoken and unseen sense of duty to future generations, if, in short, most people find you inexplicably irrational and incurably curious, then you haven't really chosen academia; rather, it has chosen you. If this is the case—and all evidence certainly suggests as much—then my letter aims not to deflect you toward more customary pursuits but rather to provide full disclosure about the road ahead. My own singular perspective may differ from yours in important ways, but I suspect I've something to offer. I have no intention of dampening your enthusiasm with boring stories of my past, though they may creep in from time to time. Rather, I hope our mutual exchanges will help me harness some of your idealism and inform my advice to you.

This much is nearly always true: Academic work is very difficult, the hours are long, and the financial rewards pale in comparison to what you could earn elsewhere. After investing in higher education for a decade-and-a-half, you'll earn a decent wage for the privilege of surrounding yourself with mostly disinterested students, intolerably jaded faculty, and woefully underpaid staff. You'll hardly be living the high life, but the national poverty line will be nowhere in sight. After six years of scrambling day and night to teach, conduct research, and write, every aspect of your professional life will be scrutinized by people who have no particular interest in your well-being. Fortunately, committee members charged with determining the worth of your professional contributions will have little interest in your personal life, in large part because they assume you don't have time for one. Thus, the decision about your tenure and continued employment will be largely professional, unless you've crossed an influential member of the faculty status committee.

Most notably, and with relatively few exceptions, decisions about your career will be based on scholarly output. In your career as a scholar, beginning as a graduate student, you are judged primarily on the basis of this one thing. Not charm, good looks, cleverness, good humor, proper perspective, optimism, integrity, or other qualities society claims as meritorious or desirable, but on scholarly output. Scientists are judged on the quantity and, to a far lesser extent, the quality of their publications. I assume artists are similarly evaluated on the basis of their art. With luck and sufficient financial sacrifice, your student loans will be paid in full by the time you are fired or granted tenure. At least, that is, the loans from your undergraduate years.

Indulge me, if you will, a personal example. A year into the second position after receipt of my doctoral degree, I was a hot commodity when I landed my first tenure-track job at Big Research University. My starting salary, as an assistant professor in 1989, was $34,000. My subsequent productivity was rewarded by early tenure and quick promotions to associate and full professor, as well as a well-deserved sabbatical leave. My scholastic output was very high, my courses drew rave reviews, and I was generating grant funds that tripled my salary. But a decade after I was hired, my salary had not kept up with inflation, and I concluded that my department head was charged with the dual tasks of destroying the department and making my life miserable. Forgetting why I love this job, I fled the ivory tower.

Frustrated and disillusioned, I took a position in a nonprofit organization that, because of historical circumstances and its size, had adopted a corporate approach to saving the world. For a year, I soaked up a thirty-percent raise and held the best job in the best nonprofit organization in the world. Within six months, I realized I'd made a mistake: The best job in the best nonprofit organization in the world, at a substantial pay increase, paled in comparison to daily interactions with the handful of students and colleagues who genuinely relish the pursuit of knowledge. Fortunately, I had followed the unsolicited advice of a colleague and dashed off a one-page memo requesting a leave of absence before I jumped from the ivory tower. I exercised my hastily constructed option to return, only a year after leaving, to a job I found woefully deficient on my way out the door.

Of course, I had no choice. I didn't choose academia nearly as much as it chose me. In his excellent book, *Letters to a Young Contrarian*, Christopher Hitchens writes that to be in opposition is something you are, not something you do. In much the same way, I am drawn to academia despite a lifetime of siren calls from other paths, most of which seem more sensible and, in some ways, more rewarding than my current pursuits.

Two promotions, two sabbatical leaves, and a leave of absence after I was hired as a baby-faced assistant professor, I'm making less money, relative to inflation, than when I started this gig sixteen years ago. And I wouldn't trade it for the world. In fact, even with all the tenure-chasing stress you're about to undergo, I'd gladly trade places with you. I envy your unbridled optimism for students and their thirst for knowledge, your own insatiable curiosity about the natural world, your naïveté about college administrators, and virtually every step of the journey before you.

We don't know what twists and turns lie ahead, of course, but we don't need to know. As the great American novelist E. L. Doctorow said when comparing writing a novel to driving a car at night, "you can see only as far as your headlights, but you can make the whole trip that way." Doctorow's comment applies to life as well as to novels and automobiles, and I know that you will embrace the winding road ahead with candor and integrity, with sympathy for those around you, and with a playful sense of adventure. You will accept adversity and ambiguity as adventure, and you will do well and be well. As Rainer Maria Rilke writes in the Ninth of his *Duino Elegies*, I eagerly anticipate seeing, "Whoever [sic] we might turn out to be at the end." Despite my uncontrolled fascination with myself (Nietzsche had me pegged), I especially look forward to seeing who you turn out to be.

Perhaps most importantly, you will not be a time-clock-punching "wage slave" like nearly all of humanity since the Industrial Revolution. In this respect, you will join writers, artists, very few other Americans, and most pre-industrial humans as a master of your own time, and you will assume membership in the dwindling leisure class. This is not the leisure class that does nothing but relax, but rather the one comprised of those who do the work they want.

I don't envy the idiocy you'll encounter on a regular basis. As a serious scholar and teacher, you will be tormented by administrators more interested in money than scholarship and by political conservatives (and neo-conservatives from the Theocratic National Party) who feel obliged to voice their concern about intellectual leftists brainwashing their progeny, despite six decades of research showing that the effects of college on attitudes, values, religiosity, and political views of students are almost nil. As if exposure to a raving teacher for a few hours each week could overcome the moral decency instilled by caring parents (try as we might). Perhaps the conservatives and neo-conservatives are nervous about the moral lessons, or the absence of them, in the academy. Or perhaps their values preclude them from recognizing a path that accentuates public service at the expense of financial gain, much less walking along it. After all, the doors of academia are open to all who are willing to forgo financial reward in exchange for a career focused on making the world a better place for future generations. Of course, I don't believe that all faculty members would—or could—be gainfully employed in the corporate world, or that they are motivated to make the world a better place, or even that those who are raking in roughly twice the national median household income to bore themselves and their students to death with the same introductory syllabus year after year would willingly pursue an alternative career. But I draw your attention to the paucity of conservatives in the fields of social work, environmental protection, and education. It is small wonder the academy is dominated by political liberals and, more importantly, intellectual liberals (not to mention liberal intellectuals).

Historically, the academy was far more liberal (i.e., broad) than it is today. A scant few centuries ago, professors were knowledgeable, broad-minded generalists who were revered for their ability to critically analyze problems. They even solved some of them. Sick people turned to professors, and appropriately called them "doctors." Eventually, the medical sciences were spun off the academy. Today, of course, medical doctors introduce themselves as real doctors and belittle the professors who spawned their discipline. You would be wise to help your attending technician solve your health problems. But don't expect to be thanked for it, and don't dare introduce yourself as "doctor" when you meet your M.D.—you'll likely trigger an unhealthy competitive streak and cause him or her to lose focus. Trust me on this one, for my sample size is large enough to reach a confident conclusion.

Mind you, I am not blaming society for its declining respect for a profession that, despite the general idealism of its members, has become increasingly irrelevant to society. The historical shift in respect from the academy to one of its recent offshoots is to be expected, given the perceived relevance of the latter and the lack of interest in the relevance of scholarship by members of the academy. Sentiment without action is, in the words of the iconoclastic Southwestern writer Ed Abbey, the ruin of the soul. And action is where we fall woefully short. The academy would be served well by attempting to recapture the spirit of liberal education it once took for granted. I fear that the spirit of liberal education—the idea of risking everything and requiring students who are able to risk everything—has died and will not return. Will we ever see humans who love the pursuit of wisdom so much they are willing to die for it? Who will serve as an individual example, and therefore keep the love of wisdom alive? If such people exist and step forward, will they come from beyond the academy, as they have before? Or will an academician stand up to society with the type of courage displayed by Socrates?

Lest you misinterpret my sentiments, I am not restricting my thoughts to the "liberal" education advanced by selective liberal-arts institutions. These institutions certainly have the right idea: They encourage voracious reading, a spirit of discovery based on inquiry, critical reflection, and the development of a whole life. They take an approach that, although being among the most liberal in the world, is far too narrow.

Liberal-arts institutions focus their educational efforts on the two broad enterprises of linguistics and logic-mathematics. Liberal-arts institutions, and the students who successfully emerge from them, excel in these two arenas. But these are merely two different types of intelligence, and there are many more. The long-time educational specialist Howard Gardner recognizes seven types of intelligence: linguistic, logical-mathematical, musical, bodily-kinesthetic, spatial, interpersonal, and intrapersonal. There could be others; in fact, these probably represent points along a multidimensional spectrum of talent. Nonetheless, we can use these seven types of intelligence to make the case that our educational efforts are too narrow.

Long before college, every student should be exposed to each of these seven arenas, and given the opportunity to excel in one or more of them. At the college level, we should continue to appreciate, rather than denigrate, multiple intelligences. Who among us—especially academicians, most of whom are laughably inept in at least five of the arenas—would not like to have passable skills in each of them? I would appreciate the knowledge and skill needed to hang a door or repair the chronically dysfunctional plumbing in my house, but talents such as these were ignored or relegated to academic "losers" in the public schools of my youth. Even more importantly, I would love to be able to express my emotions on the saxophone I abandoned in high school; unlike my plumbing, I cannot easily solve this problem by hiring a professional.

Echoing the influential American educator John Dewey, contemporary educational scholar Nel Noddings argues convincingly that all citizens should be able to surmount the minor obstacles imposed by failures in carpentry and plumbing by the time they graduate from secondary school. Better yet, she argues, we should encourage and facilitate the interests and talents of every student at every level of education, even if they do not fit the two-dimensional liberal-arts model. Yet for me, twenty years were needed before I could overcome the biases and prejudices built into our narrowly focused educational system. Two decades after graduating from high school, I finally began to appreciate and even envy the unique bodily-kinesthetic and spatial skills of my brother-in-law. My appreciation arrived long after he could fearlessly attack any home-improvement project and create a masterpiece from plywood, sheet-metal screws, and a few power tools. Meanwhile, my "superior" intellect barely allowed me to replace the float valve in my cranky toilet. Nonetheless, I found ways to look down on him from my ivory tower; for example, he could not even perform a simple multivariate analysis of variance. He seems to get along far better without this talent than I do in the absence of rudimentary bodily-kinesthetic and spatial skills.

Genuine educational reform begins with you as you encounter each student. I encourage you to know your students and their talents, to bring out the unique interests and abilities of each individual. As with every task of great import, this will be difficult. But your aptitude in the standard types of intelligence, coupled with your obsession to serve others while coaxing the best from them, assures me that you will meet the challenge with grace and good humor. I can only hope that you will inspire your colleagues to the greatness I know you will achieve.

I suspect you've felt the thrill that makes this worthwhile. Somewhere along the line, probably in one of the classes you taught to a roomful of combatively disinterested first-year students, you kindled a spark. One of those students, acting against her wishes in the face of enormous peer pressure, expressed concern about the subject you taught. She revealed her interest in the question she asked after class, the mad dash to commit your words to her notebook, or a change in body language undetected by her peers. You thought she might have been changed. And you knew you were.

That, then, to abuse the cliché, is what it's all about. If you're good enough, you will inspire your students and therefore leave an indelible mark on the world. Sure, there is other good news: You get to study what you think is important and interesting, your greatest potential health threat is either a headache or an ulcer, and you are encouraged to travel in this country and internationally. But most importantly, you get to influence inquisitive young idealists.

Admittedly, you'll rarely hear about these life-altering events. The educational enterprise lacks the instant gratification we've come to expect from contemporary American society, such that the feedback we receive about our teaching efforts is delivered in a form that is notoriously cryptic and ponderously slow. Why would we expect otherwise? After all, the best lessons we offer usually cannot be applied until our students have assumed sufficiently influential positions that their decisions reach beyond themselves and their families. Occasionally, we hear about or from one of these students from our distant past, but their voices are often unfamiliar and sometimes forgotten.

Having no other choice within the bounds of the life we've chosen (or that has chosen us), we take what we can get. Within the last decade, I clearly remember two cases in which I've changed a life, though I only met one of the students. The stories are so thrilling, if only to me, that I'll subject you to them here. I wasn't taking notes, so I am forced to paraphrase comments from all participants, including me.

"You changed my life," she said, her brown eyes glinting mischievously. (I definitely remember this quote and the sparkle in her brown eyes.) My quizzical expression left no doubt I was confused about the identity of this petite, dark-haired twenty-something. "You don't remember me, but you changed my life." She was right about one thing—I did not remember her—but at least she was not privy to my next thought: "What a way to start a semester." I had taken roll thirty minutes earlier, but matching all thirty-three names to the appropriate faces would take a few more days. So I asked the obvious: "What's your name, and how did I change your life?"

Eighteen months earlier, Jill had been majoring in sports medicine. But like many students embarking on their sophomore year, she had begun to realize that her major was poorly matched to her skills and interests. Apprehensive and unfulfilled, she searched the campus bookstore for her texts—then noticed the sign across the aisle from "Sports Medicine." She thought "Natural Resources" had a nice ring to it, and the texts appeared to focus on the outdoors, so she dialed the departmental phone number. As luck would have it, the receptionist pointed her in my direction.

I had just returned from a yearlong sabbatical leave and was brimming with enthusiasm. My lifelong interest in natural resources had been renewed and reinvigorated in the process of developing a personal mission statement and writing a book on ecology. Perhaps more importantly, I had spent a year nestled in the solitude of a city and a university a thousand miles from home. I enjoyed a year uninterrupted by teaching duties, committee assignments, and the usual disarray of academic life. I was not only enthusiastic, I was in dire need of an opportunity to share stories, chat, and generally reconnect with students. Jill could not know it, but I was a walking antidote for disenfranchised students seeking direction in life.

However, the eighteen months that had passed since my initial meeting with Jill were marked by steady decline into a post-sabbatical funk. I had come to realize that conventional measures of academic success—teaching classes, advising students, producing a steady stream of grants, journal articles, and even a book—prove insufficient for personal fulfillment. The feeling that I had failed to make a difference, that the world was not a better place for my having walked in it, had plagued me. Although I had consistently rated among the best teachers in the department, had shared my enthusiasm, and more importantly, my time, with students, I didn't really believe I was leaving a positive impression on the world.

Though she was one student whose name I could not remember moments before, Jill opened my eyes and inspired me. When I think of the mischievous gleam in her eyes, I renew a vow to make my mark though teaching and advising, one student at a time.

If you aren't inspired by the prospect of changing a life, you're in the wrong business.

The second example is even more exciting to me because it came second-hand, thereby indicating that the student not only credits me for changing his life but that he shared the story with somebody else. Yes, it was only his mother. But still.

My over-active canine companion was dragging me along her twice-daily trail one summer evening when we encountered four of her best friends: Gypsy, Josie, Senita, and Sundance, a friendly and familiar mass of misplaced slobber and wagging tails. The herd was accompanied, as always, by its middle-aged human companion. Kathy, with whom I'd only exchanged brief pleasantries in the past, shared a story relayed by a son I didn't know she had.

"My son switched majors because of you." Kathy seemed out of breath. I have enough trouble keeping track of my eight-year-old mutt, so I suspect the motley herd she follows poses a serious challenge.

"Excuse me?" Immediately, I was seeking an exit strategy, fearing her unnamed son had switched his major from my department and to another because I had offended him or expected too much from him.

"You taught his class a couple times. Something about the environment, I think. Anyway, you inspired him."

Suddenly, I found myself reveling in this story. "Oh, yes. That might be the environmental biology course in which I give a couple of guest lectures every year. I enjoy teaching that class. Please, tell me more." (One of my favorite activities is hearing good things about myself. I assume this is a universal trait.)

"He said you talked about saving the world, so he switched to environmental science." She paused for a moment, and then continued, "I think that's right. I think it's environmental science. But I don't know much about that kind of thing," she said, as if that kind of thing were an odd way to make a living.

I will long remember these two brief encounters. Reflecting on them never fails to buck me up when I'm defending my actions to bureaucrats who are interested only in avoiding litigation, or when I'm otherwise slaying administrative dragons. If you've been fortunate enough to have a similar incident, you will be hard-pressed to escape academia for long. If you haven't, I've no doubt that you will in the near future—your compassion and talent assure it. Assuming as much, I look forward to continued correspondence so that I can draw from your experiences as I reflect upon my own.

II

Your question is excellent. How and when does one know that the life of the mind is calling? I must admit that I felt no such attraction until quite recently. Indeed, I labored through many years of formal education with no particular path in mind and no urgent need to ask questions of lasting importance. I kept the blinders on through a postdoctoral position, a visiting professorship, and a decade of the tenure hunt, all the while thinking I was just doing a job. Sure, the job required attention during every waking hour. And, of course, I was driven to excel, a trait I attributed to the stamp placed on me by workaholic parents and a self-induced inferiority complex. (One definition of an academician: an egomaniac with an inferiority complex.) Consistent with the advice later offered by Harvard biologist Edward O. Wilson in his sweeping book *Consilience*, I was working at least eighty hours each week, a largely meaningless exercise I implore you to avoid. (I agree with much of Wilson's writings in this book and elsewhere, but I dislike Wilson's promotion of the type of workaholism advanced by American industry. Donald Hall's *The Academic Self* offers a far more appropriate blueprint for a well-lived life in the academy, and Hall also discusses how to determine what's expected from your institution before you arrive.)

I became obsessed with the gig only after I stepped away from it. I had to take a different position during a yearlong leave-of-absence before I realized I was hooked. The "other job" was the one I dreamed about, until I had it, as I mentioned in my last letter. Perhaps you will be called to the life of the mind somewhat earlier in life, but do not worry if you're not. Most of us are still trying to determine what we'll do when we grow up, assuming that fateful day should come. There is no hurry at your age, and perhaps not at any age. And I will not join the vast majority of my academic colleagues in assuming that a career outside the academy marks the bearer of a Ph.D. as a failure.

Even if you're not particularly interested in an academic career, a little time at just about any institution of higher education will reveal its dual mission: generation of knowledge, and transmission of it. Academicians are scholars for life, and good ones inspire others to follow a similar path of lifelong learning. But you'll be swimming upstream, especially in these times: The life of a broad-thinking intellectual requires you to be a lonely social critic, a teller of uncomfortable truths. Diogenes questioned the worth of a philosopher who hurt nobody's feelings, and I encourage your philosophical musings that mar the self-esteem of those in power. This life will require you to live at a decided slant to prevailing culture, at least at some times and places. At the extreme, it might require you to assume the title of "dissident" or at least "contrarian," in the spirit of Christopher Hitchens. Hitchens' series of letters to a young contrarian offers lucid inspiration for the life of the mind you have chosen, notwithstanding his misguided applause for American neo-colonialism. In addition to his views on dissidence, I commend to you his views on argument and religion; I will save my comments about these topics for another time.

Your latest letter mentioned the Orwellian state of the world, albeit in passing. Hitchens has much to say about George Orwell, a topic on which he is typically insightful. Personally, I am surprised Orwell's books continue to sell, steeped as they are in irony. Not because his writing is poor; to the contrary, it's superb. And not because his message is no longer relevant; it couldn't be timelier. Indeed, that's why I'm surprised: Today's facts far exceed Orwell's fiction with respect to irony. Why would the general public keep buying Orwell's deeply thoughtful books when they can more easily digest the pabulum in the daily newspaper? When the Supreme Court becomes blatantly political; when Congress becomes the lapdog of the most cognitively challenged president in history; when the executive branch assails us daily with pronouncements of "polluting the sky to clean it" and "bombing a country to save it"; and, in the name of saving the country from the bogeyman of terrorism, we are plunged into financial ruin that costs individual Americans their financial safety net, you can rest assured that irony is thriving in America. Why buy Orwell when you can get a daily dose of irony merely by reading the news?

Perhaps the two greatest ironies of our day are the failure of Americans to see the irony in which they are immersed and act on it. That's where you come in. As a member of the academic elite (there is no need to deny the inappropriately disparaging label: You are among the intellectual elite) and intellectual leftist (the two words really do belong together); you get paid to think and to educate. Why stop at the classroom when you can educate the masses? It's not as if they don't need it, even if they don't want it. Ignorance may be bliss, but bliss is vastly overrated. If bliss were the most desirable state, we would all be comfortably stoned most of the time. If you really want to make a difference in the world, set an example for your students, colleagues, and critics. The example should include criticism of the rampant stupidity, injustice, and intolerance in the world. For all the societal intolerance about race, culture, religion, sexual orientation, and myriad other harmless personal attributes (indeed, the mix of them is beneficial to society), there seems far too little intolerance of that most dangerous of traits: limited cognitive capacity.

There are many ways to reach the average sedentary American. As you might know, I speak as often as possible to citizens in groups that include nonprofit organizations and retirement communities. Countless groups meet regularly enough that they seek a fresh voice for a program, and your skill in public speaking and your ability to simplify complex issues will allow you to resonate with these groups. Avail yourself, albeit with care, to the mass media. With a little effort, you can use the media to deliver relevant messages without being sucked into the sensationalism they find so appealing. Among the easiest ways to take advantage of the media and send a carefully crafted message to a large audience is use of the op-ed feature you'll find in nearly every newspaper.

You will need to develop a thick skin to deal with the public, remembering that they seldom want to hear the truth. How else can we explain the conspicuous consumption of resources by most Americans in the face of poverty throughout the world? And not just abroad: Nearly one in five Americans live in poverty, yet a majority of Americans (admittedly a slim majority) support a plutocratic political system intent on increasing the number and proportion living in poverty while enriching the obscenely wealthy. I am no fan of folklore, but the story of the emperor's new clothes is worth knowing and repeating. Like the child who wonders why the emperor is naked, you should relish the opportunity to ask the "dumb question" and therefore expose lies and injustices that are plain to see. But unlike the fictional child, you should not expect to be tolerated with good humor when you articulate the obvious.

A story will take my advice beyond mere abstraction. It is not specifically intended to give me an opportunity to boast, though rarely can I forgo such an opening. As you might know, I was an unrepentant raconteur even before I knew about the anthropological evidence in favor of storytelling as a tool for using evidence to convince skeptics to change behaviors (note that storytelling need not involve the mysticism of folklore). But because anthropologists remind us repeatedly about the power of stories and their ability to facilitate recall, I now have evidentiary support for my habit. Stories allow us to remember concepts and facts, usually better than any other device except perhaps verse (the reason for wandering minstrels and their modern evil spawn, the annoying jingle promoting fast food). This evidentiary basis for storytelling merely assuages the minor twinge of guilt I might otherwise feel for burying you beneath a mountain of my own recollections.

This particular episode began nearly one hundred years ago, when agriculturists in the Phoenix valley lobbied for the construction of dams to irrigate their fields and for the removal of livestock from the watersheds feeding the reservoirs. The livestock were too abundant, a phenomenon consistent with the history of the western United States, and their overgrazing was causing soil erosion to a degree that threatened to fill the watershed's reservoirs with sediment. Reservoirs filled with soil, instead of water, are useless. And sediment makes a mockery of the dam. Thus the hoofed locusts threaten not only the agriculturists, but also the municipal water supply. I think you see where this is going.

The op-ed piece I submitted, which was quickly published in a Phoenix-area newspaper, called for an end to the overgrazing, at least during the ongoing drought. I avoided the most confrontational of arguments, that the entire enterprise associated with growing and eating livestock is inherently unsustainable. No need to turn off the readers, most of whom couldn't care less about future generations, in the first paragraph. And I avoided an argument based on maintenance of biological diversity because I doubt most readers care that livestock pose a threat to innumerable native species. I turned instead to the arguments with obvious appeal to the reader's selfish side. I pointed out that cattle were threatening the water and diminishing recreational opportunities in the national forest known as the Phoenix valley's playground. I couldn't pass up the

Letters to a Young Academic

opportunity to bash the neo-conservative national-level politicians who were busily promoting cattle growers at the expense of public interest. This isn't really fair, of course: Neo-cons are such an easy target they should be "off limits" for most intellectual discussions. In my defense, I was targeting readers of the op-ed page, not intellectuals. Finally, I described the collaboration between the executive and congressional branches, in blatant disregard for the separation of powers detailed in the constitution they are sworn to uphold. I expressed considerable disrespect for the nation's president, a couple of congressional representatives, and the region's cattle growers, and I asked readers to join the fray by calling any of the three in support of clean water.

Lest you have lost track of my point in this lengthy story, I was using the op-ed piece to point out the nudity of the emperor, played in this case by the region's cattle growers. The feature drew the expected knee-jerk response from my dean and department head. They were no doubt inspired by a telephone call from an "influential" (i.e., financially secure) member of the cattle growers association, perhaps the most unjustifiably powerful lobby in the American West. This is a gang that stands for the demise of cultures in the name of saving their own, for the demise of species in the name of a few dollars in their own pockets, and for the ability to keep practicing their inherently destructive way of life. They stand for their own interests at the expense of the common good. They stand, in other words, as a perfect example of the type of enterprise favored by neo-conservatives: one that abuses political power by taxing the majority to subsidize a few. Thus, they expose the neo-cons as unashamed, self-serving, power brokers who willingly trade in tomorrow for today. In stark contrast to their self-proclaimed duty to serve the people, this is the group that eagerly exchanges public good for private gain. As the public joins in, seeking something for nothing, it becomes increasingly apparent that we are instead getting nothing for everything. But I digress.

It's a neo-con world, and I suspected my opinion piece would draw the ire of my dean and, by extension, my department head. Forgetting they work for me, and I for the students, my dean and department head sided with the livestock lobby. People whose views are not supportable by logic commonly employ the tools of bully, bluster, and intimidation, and you can expect to see these tools in wide use. The point of the argument can remain unstated, as it was in this particular case. Perhaps they simply wanted to head off future attacks from the livestock lobby by making sure I was properly muzzled. Failing to find sufficient legal justification to fire me, they slithered away convinced they'd won and anxious to reprise the fight upon the occasion of my forthcoming annual performance review (which they did, in predictably illogical fashion and still unable to articulate an outcome they would find suitable, other than a muzzle on me). I neither expected nor received an apology when, eighteen months after I described contamination of the area's water supply as a potential detrimental consequence of overgrazing during a drought, more than a million people in Phoenix were forced to boil their drinking water. The newspapers blamed fires and rain, two common events on the watershed, instead of the obvious (but rarely questioned) practice of livestock grazing.

I've no doubt I'll find other ways to provoke administrators into dysfunctional and pointless arguments, and no doubt they'll be back. Agents of power rooted in ignorance always come back. You should expect them to come knocking at the door of reason with little more to offer than ridiculous arguments about hierarchy and adherence to the chain of command. I ask you to turn them away in the hope that one day they will realize how petty they appear, even if they are never able to admit how petty they've become.

I began this epistle with the folklore of the emperor's new clothes, and I encourage you to ask the obvious questions when they further justice. At the same time, I encourage you to follow the many examples of oppressed people who choose to live "as if."

I am not certain which author can claim credit for this most subversive of acts. Hitchens points, admittedly tentatively, to central Europe's Vaclav Havel and anti-nuke Cold Warrior professor E.P. Thompson, but it may well have been the Czech novelist Milan Kundera or Paul Goodman, the poet, artist, author, and eventually renowned social critic. Regardless of the source or sources, this idea is inspired and inspiring; it could well be necessary if you continue to employ your PBS mind in this decidedly MTV world.

The fundamental tenet of this approach is to live as if you are a citizen of a free society, despite considerable evidence to the contrary (evidence can be found in every application of the PATRIOT Act, the

National Security Agency's ECHELON project, and in the countless cameras and recording devices found in every city in this "free" country). Simply live as if your government believed in the Bill of Rights, as if they supported a free and democratic society, and as if they fought aggression and oppression in the name of a just, sustainable civilization. Then move beyond this simplicity by actively questioning the government and its agents who suppress the truth and oppress those who seek it. Live "as if" the oppression is not a burden to you while seeking to overcome oppression of others.

Living "as if" is the path of radicals, contrarians, and, in my dreams, all those who choose the life of the mind. Living "as if" will make your politics concrete and practical: When you encounter obstacles that interfere with you ability to live in this way, you will be forced to develop a strategy for overcoming the obstacles. Living "as if" has much to offer.

Such a life will be difficult, of course, as are all good causes. You might be worn down by the dreary weight of the seemingly endless task (*illigitimi non carborundum*), and you might not survive to enjoy many of the fruits of your labors. But by behaving literally and therefore acting ironically (i.e., by acting "as if" oppression is not oppressive), you might force those in power, in the words of Hitchens, "to act crass and then to look crass, and eventually to fall victim to stern verdicts from posterity." And how could you possibly care about a little contemporary discomfort when posterity is at stake?

By pursuing justice in your daily actions and teaching about justice and its pursuit, you can provide a shining example for your students. You can illustrate the importance and joy of intellectual activity, the justice that occasionally results, and the beauty of pursuing a life of leisure. I refer, of course, to the historical definition of leisure: doing the work one wants to do. That such a life has inherent rewards is richly satisfying and often surprising, at least to me.

III

Scholarship comes in many forms, all of them challenging, interesting, and—if you're careful to avoid obstacles to truth—fun. Scholars are like inquisitive children on intellectual treasure hunts, constantly probing the universe for answers to the big questions. Every discovery leads to more and richer questions, and every scholar stands on the shoulders of the giants who went before. (In famously inserting this phrase into a letter to fellow scientist Robert Hooke, Isaac Newton was simply repeating a phrase popularized four centuries earlier.) You can, to put a secular spin on William Blake, seek and then examine a world's worth of complexity, mystery, and beauty in a grain of sand. Of course, you must choose the correct grain of sand if you are to make the pursuit meaningful to you and humanity. This is what Newton did so well.

Not that the pursuit of truth is always fun, of course. Popular culture and its second cousin, organized religion, constantly impede the quest of knowledge and search for wisdom. I am reminded of the Catholic Church's treatment of my long-time hero, Giordano Bruno, which gave Galileo reason to recant in the face of astronomical truth. Trapped and captured by the Inquisition, Bruno was periodically interrogated during eight years of torture-laden imprisonment. Refusing to abandon the Copernican view that Earth orbits the sun instead of the converse Aristotlean (and, more importantly at the time, Catholic) view, Bruno was tongue-tied (literally) and burned alive in February of 1600. Legend, which is seldom true but which nicely embellishes a good story, has him spending his last words assailing the Church because its fear of the truth exceeded his fear of death. Copernicus, Bruno, and Galileo were right, of course, as the Church admitted a scant 392 years after murdering Bruno. In a remarkable demonstration of how quickly the Church is capable of admitting its errors and catching up to scientific facts, it concluded Charles Darwin was right about evolution only a couple years later. Perhaps in another thousand years they will admit the Jesus-as-prophet craze was just a joke that got out of hand, or, more outrageously, they will begin asking their practitioners to follow Jesus' teachings.

Unfortunately, the Church does not reward those who speak the truth today nearly as publicly as it once persecuted them, and it does not preach scientific truth nearly as vociferously as it preaches mindless mysticism. Periodic condemnation of Darwin by priests and bishops suggests that the Church is slow to educate its own leaders and that it tolerates some facts more willingly than others. But enough, for now, about the Catholic Church, which is too easy a target for those who purposely invoke reason. Furthermore, the Church's fundamentalist Protestant descendants are making even the Catholic Church seem sensible of late.

I don't mind the precepts of religion, even though religions are founded on an idea for which there is no evidence. What I mind is religious adherents living contrary to their prophets. If Christians lived as Jesus did, or as he instructed them to live, I would be a big fan of Christianity.

Our challenge could be far greater than I once imagined. I would not be the first to suggest that, just as a minority of people is incapable of distinguishing colors that are obvious to the majority, a majority is unable to differentiate between reasonable arguments and specious ones. Jonathan Singer makes perhaps the strongest argument for this case in his recent book, *The Splendid Feast of Reason*. The evidence he reviews shows rational people have not comprised a majority of any society, suggesting that rational thought lies beyond the realm of most humans. He further concludes that such "rationalists," as he calls them, comprise fewer than ten percent of American society. Singer likely is unaware that he is echoing Schopenhauer in reaching this conclusion, although Schopenhauer undoubtedly knew he was echoing Plato (another anecdote supporting Whitehead's conclusion that philosophy is a series of footnotes to Plato). Mind you, this is not about intelligence: Plenty of people who are very intelligent (by any measure) are unable to allow logic and reason to overcome irrationality. Thus, contrary to the belief and expectation of Bacon and Descartes, it would appear that efforts to unlock nature's secrets and then pass along this knowledge have become a lost cause. Indeed, "lost" might be the wrong term for it: Perhaps most people simply cannot receive and interpret the language of reason. If this is the case, as increasing evidence purports, it should be no surprise that history has treated badly the few rational people bold enough to take a firm stand in the face of an irrational majority.

The rational minority often is treated as irrational, making me wonder if assuming a rational stance is, in fact, as irrational as it is abnormal. This appears to be classic case of the inmates running the asylum, and proclaiming one's sanity is a one-way ticket to solitary confinement (from which, to begin with, rationalists are only one step removed). The impressive swiftness with which the majority has persecuted vocal proponents of reason provides plenty of cause for reflection and even retraction, which was the path taken by Galileo when faced with Bruno's fate. The title of Singer's book is well chosen, for it glorifies reason while acknowledging the rarity of its application.

Neoclassical economics assumes people act rationally, yet we know they rarely do. And the field has failed completely on every important matter: It's not called the "dismal science" for nothing. Economics could only work in the absence of war, because it presupposes the existence of law and the absence of war; the former usually has been present in America, but war is a ubiquitous feature of the country's history. Only half kidding, I use neoclassical economics as a linchpin in the argument that rational people are few and far between.

A fundamental question thus becomes: Is the inability of most people to employ reason sufficient justification to cast aside the quest for truth? What about to deny the truth? Why should we try to teach the irrational majority? Why not continue the quest for truth, enjoy the company of the rational ten percent, and leave the masses to their apparently inherent ignorance? Contrast the choices of Galileo and Bruno. As you know from our previous interactions, I find Bruno's actions particularly inspiring. And like him, I've been called contentious and ultimately self-destructive (the other common descriptor for him is "brilliant," but I've managed to avoid that label). If my appreciation for Bruno's willingness to die for the truth marks me as abnormally rational, I will wear the label with pride while readily admitting that my life is hardly in jeopardy. At least in this country, few are killed for espousing their views these days, no matter how rational those views might be. Certainly in many other places, it is much easier to die for a view, whether rational or otherwise. Some causes *are* worth dying for, even though the number of Martin Luthers pales in comparison to such virtual unknowns as Giordano Bruno. The problem with being a martyr—that one has to die for the cause—is not much of a problem after all in contemporary American society, notwithstanding recent efforts by the neoconservatives currently in power (I remind you that the ideas they are touting are neither new nor conservative; they are as old as Methuselah, as evil as any imaginable hell, and they attempt to conserve nothing except personal wealth for the inordinately wealthy). In choosing to live at a decided slant to society, I have grown accustomed to the relatively minor persecution that results from reason. Thus, the minor inconveniences faced by today's truth-tellers have so far failed to dissuade me from tilting at society's windmills.

Singer proposes science as the solution. I'd like to believe science would succeed where reason has failed, but it is difficult to maintain optimism. After all, science gave us evolution by natural selection, and overwhelming evidence has subsequently reinforced Charles Darwin's dangerous idea. Yet the American public cannot grasp the notion, with denial of the rudimentary science-based facts consistently running at seventy-five percent (among industrialized nations on this topic, none come close to American ignorance and denial of the facts). Once a mind is closed, it becomes very difficult to open with mere facts. George Lakoff, the brilliant and prolific scholar of linguistics, makes a strong case for the irrelevance of evidence with his extensive work on "framing the issues," a trick the Republican Party has perfected within the last few decades. In the spirit of bombing a village to save it, this is the gang who gives us polluting the skies to clear the air (i.e., the Clear Skies Initiative) and clear-cutting the forests to save them (i.e., the Healthy Forests Initiative). (I'm not convinced the other major party in this country—call them Business Party II—would be profoundly better than Business Party I; at most, they might stave off collapse of American society by one or two additional generations.) It seems that asking science to bail out politicians and the uninformed electorate from their lack of reason is like asking a mystic to convince a room full of scientists that a unicorn lives on the dark side of the moon.

But it appears we have no viable choice. If reason is not the answer, then the Renaissance and Enlightenment were temporary diversions along the path of absurdity and Giordano Bruno died in vain. I cannot accept mysticism as a legitimate alternative to rational thought any more than a philosopher can accept superficial thinking or a musician can tolerate improper pitch. I cannot surrender to the dual forces of ignorance and denial, though I recognize their great power.

My own trifling attempts at scholarship are centered on development of a just, sustainable human civilization rooted in environmental protection. That's a tall order, so I focus on four factors that pose great risk to the creation and maintenance of such a society: greenhouse gas emissions, consumption of resources, extinctions, and human population growth. These are the "four spikes" described by the Worldwatch Institute's Ed Ayres in his book, *God's Last Offer*. With the exception of human population, which recently started to grow "only" linearly, each of these factors is growing exponentially (i.e., "spiking" upward). Contemporary philosopher Holmes Rolston III titled his review of Ayres' book, "Four spikes, last chance," because the current generation (i.e., yours) is the last one with an opportunity to solve the massive problems posed by these global forces. Ironically, your generation is the first one to grasp the magnitude of the problems we face and the last with a chance to solve them in a way that is meaningful to future generations. Five thousand earlier generations of *Homo sapiens* contributed to these massive problems, and the half-dozen generations to occupy the planet since the Industrial Revolution owe you a big apology. Good luck collecting.

The interactions between these four factors probably are more important than the primary effect of any or all of them. As with most scholarship worthy of pursuit, articulation of the interconnections is the truly exciting part. This is where the action is because of rich complexities and the potential for genuine surprise. Any reasonably informed group of first-year undergraduate students could draw an impressive map of the interconnections between the "four spikes," although the average American citizen has not been asked to do so by his government or the mainstream news media (neither, of course, have most undergraduate students). Even worse than the ignorance of the citizenry is that any politician serious about re-election would avoid the task at any cost. Just ask Jimmy Carter.

Despite the general discomfort associated with any discussion of complex interactions, we know enough about each of the "four spikes" to act. And we must act soon if we are to avoid Armageddon. But simply having enough knowledge to act is insufficient grounds to abandon research on these topics, for several reasons. First and foremost, the neo-conservatives in charge of destroying the planet remain unconvinced that we know enough to act; apparently, we'll need to marshal even more evidence to convince them. Alternatively, perhaps they believe the evidence but are ignoring it to serve short-term goals; in this case, they will not be convinced by evidence but by the populace. (Perhaps I'm irrational or ignorant on this point, but I refuse to believe that most people are swayed by the Religious Right's argument that hastening the apocalypse, hence the second coming of Christ, is a first-rate idea. However, if they have joined forces with the neo-conservatives to destroy the New Deal and hasten the demise of American Empire in the name of the second coming for the Religious Right and massive profits for a few neo-conservatives, our cause may be hopeless in the short term. This apparently is the most likely, and most terrifying, explanation, and further evidence that betting on intelligence and rational behavior are not likely to result in much of a payoff.) Second, a decent program of education includes a serious program of research, and there is plenty of work for students and postdoctoral scholars on myriad aspects of the "four spikes." Finally, elucidation of the obvious is a time-honored tradition in academia, and I see no reason to forgo research on these most important topics merely because we know enough to act on them: Plenty of work remains to be done on the margins, if not on the big pictures. I'm sure you can think of other reasons, and I would like to know about them.

Because successfully addressing the "four spikes" underlies a just, sustainable human future, I try to base my daily actions on them, develop my courses around them, use them to provide context for my frequent guest lectures and public addresses, and target them with my research efforts. I use them to focus my scholarly efforts in two ways. First, my primary research and that of my graduate advisees explicitly focuses on retention of the planet's wealth of biological diversity. Specifically, we study the impacts from and potential controls for the many nonindigenous species that threaten native species. We also investigate historically prevalent disturbances, such as wildfire, as an ecological force. Thus, each research project addresses the extinction "spike" described by Ayres and Holmes. Second, and more recently, I have begun to focus considerable scholarly effort toward an audience broader than simply my peers and students. These synthetic efforts culminate in public addresses and books, each of which attempts to describe the connections between our daily lives and the "four spikes" while offering solutions, as well as clear-eyed descriptions of the problems.

These attempts to connect my scholarship to the lives of the general public are necessary, but obviously not sufficient. I cannot reasonably expect to turn the massive tide of American indifference toward future generations and nonhuman species without considerable assistance from you and a battalion of like-minded individuals. Even this might not be enough, though I'm not ready to give up on my idealistic dream of environmental protection and social equity. This dream begs for a rational worldview deeply rooted in facts and inspired by the natural world.

Facts are not enough, of course. Michigan Congressman John Dingell reportedly was among the first public officials to take this view to its extreme form in claiming that the facts, although interesting, are irrelevant. I reluctantly agree that important social and political issues cannot be tackled with facts alone, though I refuse to give up completely on rational empiricism. Even if the pragmatist philosophers are correct that we observe a map of the landscape rather than the landscape itself, our observations of the map should provide more bases for our decisions than phenomena that cannot be observed. I am unwilling to pursue the route of mystics who rely on "ways of knowing" rooted in spirituality and therefore unfiltered feelings, unchecked emotions, and unseen spirits as foundations for our decisions. Nor am I suggesting we close our minds. But our minds should not be kept so open that our brains fall out, to borrow a phrase from the British evolutionary biologist Richard Dawkins. Like Dawkins, you should use your position in the academy to pursue and promote scholarship rooted in reason, even when the results generate controversy.

Passion, unlike spirituality, can and should be kindled in defense of informed decision-making. Passion should fire the imagination and drive the pursuit of social justice and environmental protection. Well-placed fervor in defense of justice and oppressed societies depends, in part, on inspiration in the forms of art, music, and literature. The connection between these issues is rich scholarly terrain for the type of unity humans pursued for four centuries before abandoning it within the last three decades. As Harvard biologist Edward O. Wilson points out so eloquently in *Consilience*, uniting the sciences and the humanities underpins the development of a just, sustainable human civilization. Such unity depends on scholarly efforts in the classroom and beyond. Wilson is not the first thinker to be tormented by a desire for unity. Indeed, the first words of *Consilience* directly quote Francis Bacon, and the idea of unifying knowledge dates at least to Plato. According to philosopher of science George Horton, people who seriously pursue such unity have no choice; mental anguish results from failure to pursue the passion for unity of knowledge.

As you know, products of my scholarship offend some members of the public and also, on a recurring basis, my supervisors. Most of us want clean air and clean water, but a few people do not. Most of us want to keep poisons out of our food and assault weapons off the streets, but a few people are enriched—albeit only financially—by taking the opposite path. I have to believe that most of us want to defend the public good, but I also know that a few people would prefer to plunder the common good for personal gain. Tack on the inability of many people to behave rationally, and it should come as no surprise that I offend some. Given the frequency with which I criticize the majority of Americans, if only indirectly, I'm surprised and sometimes disturbed that I haven't yet managed to offend more. I realize that their lack of offense may simply reflect ingrained apathy toward reacting "against" something as much as "for" something. Rodney King once famously asked, "Can't we all just get along?" In fact, generally we do, if only because most of us can't be bothered to disagree. A couple of examples suggest the type of response you can expect from scholarly efforts that criticize society and its citizens, although even these feeble responses occur far too infrequently. The point of these examples is not to illustrate my propensity for offending others (though that gives me sufficient pleasure to suggest a pathology), but that you should not shy away from controversial scholarship. It's what we've done that makes us who we are, to mangle a phrase crooned by Jim Croce, the eloquent folk singer from my generation. If Croce was correct, perhaps I'm an equal-opportunity offender.

I recently penned an op-ed piece on global warming. The article called attention to the considerable havoc wreaked on the planet's organisms, including those of our own species, by the actions of a few. Notably, many of the offenders are Americans whereas most of the sufferers occupy foreign lands. The potential consequences of global warming for current and future generations of human beings are unmatched by anything humanity has ever seen.

Sadly, our political "leaders" have yet to seriously consider actions that might stem the tide of impending, global-scale disaster.

The hate mail arrived almost immediately, appearing in my e-mail inbox within a few hours of the paper's printing. Pretty impressive stuff, considering my e-mail address was not included with the article. Such is the power of the technology. (Which reminds me of an unforeseen benefit of the Internet: It has unmistakably disproved the old expression, "A million monkeys at a million typewriters could reproduce Shakespeare.")

I responded in rational fashion to each piece of mail, and invited the authors to attend my classes. They haven't shown, yet.

I mentioned another recent example in my last letter to you. This was the defense of the livestock industry by my supervisors when I questioned the ridiculous practice of attempting to grow cows in deserts of the American Southwest during a drought.

These minor examples demonstrate the type of inconvenience produced by scholarship that sheds light on the typical American's lifestyle. Each cost me a few hours and an indeterminate amount of political capital, both of which seem a small price for the resulting fun, excitement, and potential usefulness. Thus, I recommend you pursue similarly exciting and potentially useful scholarship throughout your career, even though your closest colleagues likely will be privately supportive and publicly inconspicuous. (If your experiences match mine, lack of courage will render moot your colleagues; eyes downward, they oppose in public the ideas they support in private).

Nonetheless, it is with some hesitation that I recommend you pursue justice and sustainability beyond publication of your scholarship in the respected obscurity of refereed journals, for such action could cost you a wonderful job in an intellectually stimulating environment. And, of course, there is considerable variability among institutions: those that focus on the liberal arts tend to tolerate and might even reward scholarship that is inappropriately denigrated at large research universities. In any case, if you wait until you have tenure to save humanity from itself, you might be too late. The task is far greater than you or I, and either of us may better serve the cause by dropping out of the academic race to become a labor organizer or a leftist politician. Indeed, an exceptional waiter can create more social and political change than the average academician. I see no reason to let the waiters have all the fun.

IV

Socrates notwithstanding, higher education has been a teacher-centered activity for the last few centuries. You are perhaps too young to remember the strictest application of this model, in which the professor was viewed as a man (because they nearly always were men) of considerable wisdom by his students, who were ingloriously termed "pupils" (the Latin root for which means "child"). Generations of unabashed amateurs basked in the reflected glory of the "sage on the stage."

Then came the 1960s, replete with social unrest that challenged authority and, in many cases, mocked it. Actually, with the exception of student-led protests on many college campuses, the 1960s reached academia in the 1970s because institutions of higher learning are so slow to change course. But when authority finally was turned on its pointy little head, colleges and universities around the country reversed direction.

As with the purported arrival of the 1960s, the reversal of pedagogic direction was considerably more complicated in reality than in the history books. Colleges and universities *claimed* to reverse direction, heralding themselves as student-centered institutions in countless brochures and catalogs, and eventually on websites. These claims were the product of research on "active" and "inquiry-based" learning, much of which supported the notion that retention of material was lower for lectures than any other teaching style. The claims also resulted from the marketing programs that appeared in virtually all colleges and universities as they found themselves competing for the "best and brightest" students. Marketing claims aside, the continued presence of the same tenured teachers in the same classrooms teaching the same courses was hardly conducive to a sea of change in technique. Thus, with the exception of new faculty trickling into the academy— a snail's-pace process, in part, because senior academicians are loath to retire—the "student-centered" educational model trumpeted by colleges and universities had little to do with activities in the classrooms.

And that's probably a good thing.

The concept of "professor as guide" for the self-motivated student might represent a noble model if your students are truly hungry for knowledge and blessed with sufficient skill, maturity, and curiosity to seek knowledge for its own sake. But for the most part, this model represents a bad case of New Age pandering. It is consistent with the idea of students as customers, an idea that peaked (briefly, thankfully) with a Total Quality Assurance (TQA, sometimes termed Total Quality Management, TQM) model in many universities in the 1980s and 1990s. Customers are supposed to have full knowledge of the products they are purchasing; in contrast, the typical student has virtually no knowledge of disparate disciplines, colleges, or even himself when he meanders onto campus at the tender age of eighteen. It is difficult to imagine many students making significant contributions to courses in medieval history, for example, compared to a professor who has written books on the subject. There are other flaws with the TQA/TQM model, including an intractable inability to quantify learning that endures beyond the current semester, difficulty in developing a meaningful system by which to rank colleges and universities, and failure to acknowledge that the college experience is not an instantly marketable commodity that has explicit, universal value.

Collectively, these shortfalls suggest that the concept of "students as customers" has little utility. A more appropriate model, if students were truly literate and interested, would treat them like patients and professors like doctors. That is, students would be inherently interested in their intellectual health, and doctors would provide advice and present options for enhancing their knowledge. Adopting this model immediately suggests intensive care as the relevant domain, as pointed out by graduate-school dean Phillip Shelley in a January 2005 commentary in the *Chronicle of Higher Education*. Shelley astutely observed that most college students are poorly prepared to solicit advice from professors and even more poorly prepared to accept the advice and use it to change their own knowledge and values.

My criticism of the student-centered model does not suggest that we construct barriers between teachers and students either in the classroom or outside it. We cannot help students achieve their hopes and dreams if we do not know what they are. Therefore, we must know who they are, with what they struggle, and whom they aspire to become. We must keep the dreams of our students foremost in our minds as we set goals for them. But acting as if students are the focus of a course on Roman history,

Australian aboriginal culture, or conservation biology is neither necessary nor particularly helpful in the realization of their dreams. Placing the student front and center, and therefore suggesting that he is the most important element of classroom discourse, can interfere with integration of lasting knowledge; appreciation for alternative lifestyles, cultures, and species; and development of critical-thinking skills fundamental to a moral education. And placing students' interests first leads inevitably to evaluation of faculty by students, and then to uncritical adoption of the assessment results by unthinking administrators.

I have no illusions that the typical university administrator can distinguish between anecdotal evidence from a questionable source and the hard evidence of scholarship and its products, or that he would even want to. Nor do I mean to suggest that every administrator is typically short sighted and oblivious to genuine scholarship. In my two-decade career, I have already met three university administrators who kept their eyes on the scholastic ball: They went to work every day to work hard on behalf of faculty and students, and the consequently earned the respect of faculty, students, and other administrators.

If the teacher-centered approach to higher education has been discredited by a large body of contemporary research, and the student-centered approach does not offer a general solution, it seems our educational efforts are left with only one viable target: the subject. The relevant model for higher education is one focused squarely on the subject, as championed by one of the gurus of contemporary educational thought, Parker Palmer. This model is consistent with the approach employed for generations in Europe and the United States by visionaries, such as Frederick William Sanderson, the longtime head of England's Oundle School, who unwaveringly promoted cooperation among students (vs. competition), and steadfastly insisted that every door on campus remain open at all times, thus allowing ready access to libraries and laboratories when inspiration struck.

According to the subject-centered model, teachers and students comprise a corps of discovery in which each individual is expected to make contributions to the success of the team of learners. This model might not be particularly effective for pre-college learning because students have acquired too few life experiences and too little maturity to make meaningful contributions. But at the college level, we must assume that learners are adults. I have interacted with many students who have traveled more broadly than I, and none who have traveled to the same places and accumulated the same experiences. The collective body of knowledge and experiences in a single classroom often is impressive, and usually is largely untapped. Allow me an example.

I recently taught a course in conservation biology at a large research university to about thirty students, most of them juniors and seniors. As with all of my courses, I expected the students to interact thoughtfully with other members of the class. But I knew they would resist: Because they had spent a few years at this large state university, the very ideas of thinking and interacting were foreign to most of them. Overcoming their fear of saying something "stupid" in the midst of their peers posed a daunting challenge, but a first-day icebreaker, patience, persistence, repeated appeals to a spirit of cooperation, and a role-playing exercise within the first week or two forced their collective hands (and mouths and brains, too).

By the third week of a fifteen-week course, contributions were coming from every quarter of the class. Matthew worked full-time for a local nonprofit conservation organization, which explained his vast knowledge of legal and political aspects of conservation, and perhaps also his boundless energy and perennial five o'clock shadow. Ever-cheerful forty-year-old Dana had worked for two national nonprofit conservation organizations, and she had considerable experience with the applied aspects of conservation biology. Brian, a twenty-year-old premedical student, spent every spare moment hunting, fishing, and hiking, so he was more interested in, and knowledgeable about, local ecosystems than just about anybody I'd met. The anthropological backgrounds of two students made them sensitive to and informed about disparate cultural perspectives about non-human species. Nearly half the students had traveled to "lesser-developed" countries, which gave them considerable insight into the nether world of conservation policies and practices. I could go on (and on, as you have observed). In short, every student was able—and, in a relatively short time, willing—to make contributions that advanced the knowledge of the entire group. Because I was teaching this course for the first time, I suspect I learned more than any student in the class. It perfectly exemplified what I tell every class upon our first meeting: "I am here to learn, and I trust you are, too."

One could argue that a focus on the subject is a small and natural extension of a focus on the student, a minor step beyond professor as guide. That is, this approach might not contradict the notion of "guide on the side." I cannot deny the charge except to note that small steps often produce large changes.

Active, learner-constructed knowledge also can result from independent research. Such research can be conducted within the context of virtually any curriculum.

I always admit, on the first day of class, that I don't know all there is to know about the subject I'm teaching. Better yet (though I suspect many students and most parents think it's worse), I admit that I'll be learning along with students, that the exorbitant price of tuition does not guarantee an "answer" from me. This brings to mind a quote from A. J. Scott's 1852 inaugural address at Owens College, where he was the first principal: "He who learns from one occupied in learning, drinks from a running stream. He who learns from one who has learned all he is to teach, drinks 'the green mantle of the stagnant pool.'" Scott is quoting The Bard's *King Lear*, a seemingly endless fountain of inspiration and irony.

I have come to believe that a sharp focus on the subject will lead to learning for all, to the betterment of the learners and the discipline. The spirit of intellectual adventure within our corps of discovery might be whetted, but seldom is it sated. As a result, students are committed to learning outside the classroom and beyond the semester's end. That I don't have the correct answer for every question we encounter throughout a semester seems a small price to pay for stoking an adventure that never ends. And it means nobody has to drink scum off a stagnant pond.

V

How, specifically, can we draw from the uniqueness of each student to enhance learning by all? How can we reward each student's individuality in the classroom, and outside it? I have a few suggestions, though I recognize they are insufficiently small. There are many more techniques I have not yet tried, a failing I attribute to general sloth on my own part. I hope you can modify the ones I've tried for your own use. More selfishly, I hope you will let me know how you enhance learning and reward individuality. What works for you?

To recognize and reward uniqueness, we must first know each student. Each student is unique, as ensured by the wonder of DNA. The potential people who could be sitting in any classroom chair but who will never exist outnumber the atoms in our universe. Good teaching recognizes, highlights, and rewards the unique contributions of each individual. To add to the daunting task, we fight for an oncoming and ill-defined future in students we barely know while, as the educator and philosopher John Dewey observed, the students themselves lust for action in the here and now. Forestalling student demand for action today with promises of the "good life" in the form of a well-lived future is a great challenge; it partially explains why anthropologist Loren Eiseley described teaching thusly in *The Night Country*: "There is no more dangerous occupation on the planet, for what we conceive as our masterpiece may appear out of time to mock us—a horrible caricature of ourselves."

In an attempt to learn about the students in my classes, I begin every semester by taking each student's photograph, which I ask him or her to label with the name they prefer. I study these "flash" cards so that I can call each student by name on the second class period (online photographs at some institutions negate this step, but my university has not made this investment). This is a small step, and knowing a name is not the same as knowing a person. It is a necessary first step along a journey that recognizes, and revels in, individuality.

By arriving early and staying late for each class period, I have opportunities to chat with students about the class and their lives. And I make myself available to meet with them at times that work for them, to every possible extent. Formally posting office hours is a joke if you are not willing to actually know the student with whom you are visiting.

Also on the first day of class, I read a statement, some version of which appears on the website for each class I teach: "Because I want you to learn new things about yourself and about life, I will award credit for doing something substantive you have never done before (eating a new menu item at Taco Bell does not qualify as substantive; if in doubt, please ask). I will award up to two points for each new experience, and you are limited to three new experiences each week during the semester. Each new experience must be described in a single paragraph." The idea, like nearly all the "innovations" I employ, is borrowed (in this case, from the creative writer and instructor of writing, Derrick Jensen).

You might argue that this is a "gimme," that a student can earn points simply for living. I can't argue with that, nor would I want to. Some might suggest that students will cheat, claiming they've had a new experience when they haven't. I have no idea how to account for this argument, other than hoping that grades based on five hundred points mitigate the potential for cheating on the basis of two measly points (optimism prohibits thinking about those who would repeat the offense each week). I've also heard arguments about earning points that have nothing to do with the topic of the class, that a student should not be able to transform a C to a B in Conservation Biology for skydiving and other extracurricular activities. I've many responses to this argument.

For starters, college is about learning, including experiential learning, to a far greater extent than it is about grades. Rewarding experiences beyond the classroom provides an opportunity to reiterate that point. In addition, I think many new experiences are more important to an individual's life than much of what we learn about conservation biology. Living broadly by trying new activities is hugely important and deeply enriching to development of a whole life. I encourage students to share their experiences with each other, thus contributing to a spirit of community in the classroom (Ernest Boyer, the ultimate advocate of campus community, would love this response). Further, I connect most of the student's experiences beyond the classroom to conservation biology, and I encourage them to do the same. Skydiving, for example, provides a fresh perspective on the world around us; it also encourages confrontation of fear, something we all can benefit from now and then. Writing about skydiving provides additional practice with written communication, and none of us gets enough of that. I always reward the points for substantive experiences, and my attentive editing reinforces the importance of writing well.

For all group activities, in class and beyond, I make every effort to maximize heterogeneity within groups. Mixing students with different ethnic and cultural backgrounds, majors, ages, and interests allows them to learn from each other, and not just about the stated topic of the day's class. In hearing the views of others and interacting with "different" people, students learn from their peers and confront their prejudices.

In constructing examinations, I strive to incorporate questions that address all levels of Bloom's taxonomy and account for different styles of learning, at least in the broad sense Bloom intended. To minimize test anxiety, I allow several hours for exams that should be completed in forty minutes. In addition, I use an examination format that rewards cooperation and communication, the details of which I will provide in a future letter. And I work very hard to reward the process by which a student formulates his answer, in addition to the answer itself; many of my questions have several "right" answers and processes by which the "right" answer can be reached. I am swayed by seemingly indefensible views supported by strong logic to a far greater extent than by the bleating of thoughtless sheep that simply regurgitate my own views. In short, I attempt to reward those who think, even if their thoughts are different from mine.

Perhaps the strangest assignment I give, in the eyes of my colleagues, is a work of art or literature (each student decides which he or she will prepare). Specifically, I require each student to prepare a significant piece of art or literature that addresses a topic (or topics) discussed in class. I am neither an artist nor a literary scholar, which suggests that I might not be the best judge of these projects. So I grade liberally, using criteria developed for each project by its creator. I also require the student to grade his own project, using criteria he developed, and I use my grade and his to determine the final grade. Remember, it's about learning, not grading (or, in the words of the Buddha, "look at the moon, not the finger"). The students usually are hesitant, at least in the beginning. Years of science courses have destroyed, rather than encouraged, their collective creativity. And it does not help when the occasional guest lecturer or adviser reminds them: "If you're finger painting, you're not doing science." But beyond the students' initial hesitation lie talent, passion, and enthusiasm. Each year, I am humbled by the effort of the students and inspired by their works, which routinely include quilts, sculpture, photography, poetry, and music.

I have toyed with the practice of individualized contracts in which each student develops his own set of assignments and examinations. My few attempts to employ this approach have left me quite disappointed by the lack of creativity displayed by students. They tend to focus on the things I think do not matter much or that are very difficult to quantify. Besides, even for a class of thirty or fewer students, this is a real pain in the ass. As a result, I have targeted individualized instruction in other ways.

Among my greatest joys are working with graduate students and occasional undergraduate students who display interest in the scholarship I find so riveting. As a result, much of my time is spent thinking about or advising these self-motivated students whose research projects are, by definition, highly individualized. In particular, I support thesis and dissertation projects that fit the passions and talents of each student. And I have, albeit recently, become much better at encouraging individuality beyond the university experience. A minor example should explain how I am trying to support an increasingly liberal worldview.

One of my graduate advisees has a strong personal interest in Brazil. She visited the country in high school, and has maintained her interest in part by practicing Portuguese and participating in *capoeira*, a Brazilian form of martial arts. She conducts field research on ecosystems in North America that are similar to those found in Brazil; by her own admission, this is a small stick on a rather large bonfire of interest.

A few years ago, Erika spent the summer in Brazil. She spent half the summer helping teach a course in field biology, the other half traveling and soaking up Brazilian culture. Though I tried unsuccessfully to hide it, I was unhappy she spent several weeks touring when she could have been working on her dissertation research. Envy played its hand, as well: I've still never been to South America or much anywhere else. A few of my colleagues made no attempt to hide their displeasure to Erika or to me for "letting" her go. Apparently, they failed to notice she's an adult.

She went the following summer, too, by which time the idea had started to grow on me. I encouraged her to go the next summer, though it's not as if I could have stopped her. Somewhere along the line, I realized that life is more important than a Ph.D. dissertation. Immersing oneself in another culture is far more important than immersing oneself in data analysis.

Despite my advanced age, it appears I'm capable of learning life's important lessons, even from students twenty years younger than I.

VI

Considerable evidence indicates that modern American universities have fallen prey to the Lake Wobegon effect, in which all students are above average. In the case of university students and the grades they receive, all students are not merely above average; they are brilliant enough to avoid any grade below a B. At most universities, half the students are rated excellent in nearly every class. The sham of grade inflation is detrimental to institutions of higher education, to society, and to students. Grade inflation violates the social contract between our institutions and society. When we never award failing grades, passing grades become meaningless. And when we only award exceptional grades, regardless of performance, the public rightfully loses confidence in our integrity. When academic institutions or the individuals comprising them lose integrity, are they left with any worthy attributes?

The goal is not to help students meet increasingly lower standards: We must reverse this race to the bottom. Currently, one in seven college graduates is functionally illiterate, a statistic variously attributed to parents, public schools, or unappreciated and under-funded educational initiatives pushed by the neo-conservatives who have co-opted the country's political agenda. Rather than assigning blame and lowering standards so that any warm body can meet them, the goal must be to help students meet rigorous academic standards. In the short term, this will require exceptional dedication on behalf of the academy and perhaps fewer courses for each student. In the long haul, raising the bar and helping students clear it will require resources the neo-conservatives are unwilling to provide.

Students suffer when we do them the disservice of granting grades they have not earned. Consider the case of playwright and screenwriter Aaron Sorkin, who spoke to the 1997 graduating class at his alma mater, Syracuse University. The *Chronicle of Higher Education*, a weekly newspaper I commend to you strongly, reported the uplifting story of his failure and subsequent rejuvenation:

> As a freshman, part of my core requirement was to take a class with Professor Geri Clark. . . . We read and discussed two plays a week. . . . The problem was that the class met at 8:30 in the morning . . . and all this going to class and reading was having a negative effect on my social life in general and my sleeping in particular. At one point, being quizzed on *Death of a Salesman*, a play I had not read, I gave an answer that indicated I wasn't aware that at the end of the play, the salesman dies.
>
> And I failed the class. And this had consequences. It not only meant I would have to repeat the class my sophomore year, but in the drama department, students aren't allowed to perform until they've completed Freshman Core, and so the F in Geri's class meant I wouldn't be on the stage for another year, and that was seismic. It was the low point in my life. It was depressing, frustrating, and infuriating.
>
> And it was, without a doubt . . . the single most significant event that has occurred in my evolution as a playwright.

I came to my sophomore year, and I went to class, and I paid attention; and we read Aristotle and I paid attention. Something was happening to me in class, and I didn't know what it was at the time, but I was paying attention.

I have stood at the back of the Eisenhower Theater at the Kennedy Center in Washington, watching a pre-Broadway tryout performance of my play, knowing that when the curtain came down I could go back to my hotel room and fix the problem in the second act with the tools that Geri Clark gave me.

Four years ago I was introduced to Arthur Miller at a Dramatists Guild function, and we spent a good part of the evening talking. A few weeks later, when he came down with the flu, he called me and asked me if I would fill in for a day as a lecturer in the City University of New York. The subject was *Death of a Salesman* . . .

When I give interviews, and the interviewer asks me what my big break was, I tell them it was the day Geri Clark flunked me and said, "Come back and pay attention next time."

Like Geri Clark, I have given failing grades to students who did not meet my high expectations. As you might expect, I've been frustrated by a department head and peers who think I'm an uncaring, unfeeling automaton. These "colleagues," including my department head, have asked me to pass students because they "need this class to graduate." And I've had the pleasure of seeing my adherence to principle rewarded in two ways. First and most importantly, students have returned to my class and passed, thereby elevating their confidence in themselves and the institution. Mastery of a difficult challenge inspires confidence and enhances moral fiber. In contrast, there is no glory and little honor in accomplishing an easy task. Second, my peers voted to award a degree to a student who failed my course three times: They changed the requirements of the degree before I abandoned my principles and lowered my standards to match theirs. Sticking to one's principles is hardly a death-defying act, as it was for Bruno and Galileo. Still, it brings a modest dose of pleasure to be granted a small victory after standing alone on the side of principle. Had I been proved right instead of merely stubborn, I would feel even better.

Let me be clear: I take no pleasure in failing any student, much less the same student on multiple occasions. I take partial responsibility for a student who fails any of my courses. But I cannot take responsibility for the actions of others, including students who give too little effort and peers who want to lower the bar.

How, then, do we ensure that our classes are rigorous? How do we challenge each student to take up the gauntlet and challenge not only himself, but other class members and—of course—us? I will suggest a few things before turning to the most important issue; on that, I seek your advice.

First and foremost, I return each graded exercise the class period after it is due. This is often challenging because nearly everything else is more alluring than grading papers. So when the semester begins, I schedule time for grading on my calendar after each exam and assignment. Maximum learning is achieved with immediate feedback, and this is as close to "immediate" as I am able to achieve in most cases. Students will know you care about them if you return each graded exercise promptly, and they are far more likely to care about the subject if they know you care about them. As Nel Noddings frequently reminds us in her books on lifelong education, "care" is a reciprocal enterprise.

The students should not be devastated when the exercise is returned. We can grade critically without being caustic, and we should. Every submission has good qualities, and you should find them, point them out, and hold them up for praise. Each student should know he did something well, and that you found it and recognized its value. The worst of papers has redeeming qualities and the best has problems. Students do not learn if they turn off the intellectual switch upon seeing a caustic comment on the first page. Actually, they do learn: They learn about power and pettiness while questioning their own self-worth.

An even simpler way to avoid devastation is to use a "no surprises" approach to returning assignments. You can take a lot of pressure off you and your students by using any number of techniques to let them know ahead of time how well they performed. I particularly like to use a cooperative exam, administered to small groups of students, immediately after or instead of an exam for each individual student. I described the format for these exams in a recent letter.

I use a blind-grading scheme for all exams and most other assignments. Students submit exams and assignments under an alias known only to them, and they change aliases for each new submission. As I return the material, each student tells me his or her alias and I record the name alongside the alias. Each semester, the first exam contains surprises: the pale-skinned "Goth girl" clad in black who sneaks in late for class and then slouches half-asleep in the back of the room earns the highest grade without ever taking a note or displaying any interest in the class, while the inquisitive, engaged, and engaging young man who always arrives early and stays late to ask questions somehow fails the exam. Had I known who they were when I was grading, I could have given the latter the benefit of the doubt in interpreting his response to a question or, worse yet, assumed the Goth girl was merely guessing and therefore scored her exam harshly. As with most actions that reduce inequity, blind grading poses logistical challenges and has trade-offs. For example, I cannot use graded material to familiarize myself with each student because I do not know the source of written comments. As a result, I am developing myriad other methods to acquaint myself with students. Despite these minor shortcomings, I am convinced that blind grading is a small but worthwhile step toward equity, and I've yet to encounter a student who disagrees.

In addition to blind grading, I sometimes mark and return papers with detailed comments and suggestions, but with no grade. I grade the papers, and tell the students I've done so, but I do not reveal the grades until they've had a chance to grade their own work, usually by the next class period. Usually, they are tougher on themselves than most teachers, including me, so this is not nearly as risky as it might seem. It democratizes the grading process while providing an opportunity for learning to occur (which is, remember, the point): Students seem more willing to study the instructor's comments when they are grading their own papers. And I am willing to change the grade I've assigned if a student's justification for a higher grade is sufficiently compelling.

Finally, I grade each assignment on the basis of good writing skills. To this extent, each of my classes is a writing class. Do we not expect our students to graduate with good ideas *and* the ability to express them? Few of our students will establish themselves as brilliant practitioners in their respective fields. But all of them should have sufficient communication skills to interact positively with other professionals and the general public, both orally and in writing. An example of the importance of writing (and speaking) is provided by George Lakoff, the linguist I mentioned in an earlier letter, who points out the success of the Republican Party in "framing the issues" with misleading language. As a result of my focus on development of communication skills, I demand that students participate in each class meeting, and I make it easy for them to participate; I particularly focus my efforts on students who have a limited ability to articulate their thoughts, and often I am inspired by their progress during a single semester (and, if they are to be believed, so are they).

None of the preceding discussion is intended to suggest that I enjoy grades or grading; I despise the standardized version of grades routinely implemented, indeed required, by the institutions at which I've worked. They assume that all students have equal talents, interests, and ambitions, and that an A for one is the same as an A for another.

They assume that standardized schemes of grading are fair, when clearly they are not. I have struggled mightily with this concept, with little to show for it. This, then, is the important issue to which I alluded earlier. How do we reward those students who give all they are able, yet fail to produce magnificent works? How do we acknowledge the Herculean efforts of the cognitively challenged when their best efforts result in scores lower than those of their peers? Perhaps an example will clarify my point.

I am severely chromatically challenged, as you know. When I asked my completely humorless optometrist to categorize my color-blindness, he let me know, in no uncertain terms, that, "You are deficient throughout the spectrum." I can only assume he was talking about my vision, and not my life, for he knows little about the latter. How do we adjust our grades for those who capable of seeing only shades of gray, rather than the full palette of cognitive colors? How do we fairly reward those who meet their potential while recognizing that some students have little capacity for linguistics and logic-mathematics, the only "brands" of intelligence acknowledged by the American educational system?

I am haunted by this problem. Perhaps we should accept the limitations of our educational system and simply fail the students who do not meet our high standards, steeped as they are in a uniquely Anglo perspective that concentrates exclusively on linguistics and logic-mathematics. Perhaps Jules Henry's 1963 book *Culture Against Man* was right on target with its devastating critique of American educational institutions (although his own grammar was less than perfect): "School is indeed a training for later life not because it teaches the 3 Rs (more or less), but because it instills the essential cultural nightmare fear of failure, envy of success, and absurdity." Consistent with Henry's interpretation, I have employed the traditional approach of grading in a manner reflective of our nightmarish culture, that is, in a manner consistent with my university's expectations. I have grown increasingly uneasy about this approach, and not simply because American culture is a nightmare. For example, the students who fall off the university bandwagon are overwhelmingly ethnic minorities or counter-culture citizens. This, by itself, should give us reason to pause and reflect, if only because these are the people who might yet save us from ourselves. The United States of Advertising, as investigative satirist Paul Krassner calls us, is a difficult country in which to live for those who look or act too differently from the masses. The herd sniffs warily at the strange ones among us.

But simply adopting the standard scheme of grading fails to recognize, much less reward, exceptional students. Einstein's difficulties in mathematics come to mind, but I often wonder how well Charles Darwin, Henry David Thoreau, or Herman Melville would have performed on contemporary standardized examinations, such as the SAT or ACT. These exams attempt to evaluate the lowest common denominator of literacy, but they make no attempt to evaluate genius. Perhaps this is not the point of higher education. But then, what is?

As always, I look forward to your response. I welcome your insights.

VII

According to Louis Schmier, Valdosta's inspiring teacher and philosopher, "Education boils down to acquiring the desire, confidence, and courage to question the answers." Good teaching instills these traits, thereby encouraging students to pursue a life of intellectual inquiry. Such inquiry requires that each of us admit our ignorance, and relish the opportunity to overcome it. We are all ignorant, albeit about different things. Learning from each other allows us to employ collective action in the battle against individual ignorance.

Whether two heads are better than one depends on the heads in question. But it is difficult to imagine a scenario in which a dozen humble, appropriately motivated heads are not better than one. This is essentially the idea of a "corps of discovery" to which I referred in my description of subject-centered education, but with a good dose of humility tossed in to the mix.

As I mentioned earlier, the "sage on the stage" philosophy of teaching has been largely abandoned by contemporary educators in this country (if not in China, Africa, and England), in part because students do not learn particularly well from this approach. In addition, there is every reason to believe we can all learn more by starting from a point of humility that recognizes and values knowledge from all points in the classroom. If you are more intelligent than students in some sense, you likely are less intelligent than some of them in many other arenas. For the most part, it is your persistence rather than your intellect that is rewarded by a position in academia.

With that in mind, I encourage you to remember who works for whom in the academy. For starters, you serve the students (and through your scholarship, the remainder of society), and so on, down to the university president. You will not be surprised to learn that administrators often forget how this works: As you've likely heard, power corrupts, thereby turning educational hierarchy on its head. Ideally, a department head works at making it easy for you to work for your students. (In my case, the opposite is true. But I know there are department heads who follow this model.) Higher-level administrators, in turn, work for the administrators "below" them on the organization chart, securing funding, buildings, and infrastructure to support higher learning.

What is higher learning? My favorite definition was provided by Thomas Angelo in a 1993 issue of the bulletin of the American Association of Higher Education: "Higher learning is an active, interactive, self-aware process that results in meaningful, long-lasting changes in knowledge, understanding, skills, behaviors, attitudes, beliefs, opinions and/or values—that can *not* be attributed primarily to maturation." This seems a reasonable definition for all education, instead of simply the "higher" variety.

The goal, according to this view, is to produce long-lasting change in our students. Notice that knowledge and skills represent only a portion of higher education's broad goal. Ultimately, the primary focus is on changes well below the surface: understanding, behaviors, attitudes, beliefs, opinions, and values. If all goes according to plan, we change ourselves in the process of changing our students. In the best of all possible worlds, we all learn empathy, that rarest of attributes that, in sufficient quantities, would eliminate racism, sexism, inequity, poverty, and war from the planet. Personally, I've rarely had an argument or taught a class in which I was not changed by the experience.

As with much of what we do, when we are acting in the best interests of our students, we will meet considerable resistance. The difficulty and discomfort associated with learning makes many people quite averse to it. Further, as former President Bill Clinton used to say, "People like change in general, but not in particular." Most people especially dislike changes that strike closest to them, and there is little doubt that learning is on this list. Perhaps the best we can hope for is to serve as role models, reveling in the experience of learning and hoping students will follow.

One specific role we can serve is that of inquisitor (with a small "i"). By constantly probing, and encouraging students to do the same, we often discover that we know more than we first imagined, especially collectively. In addition, the practice of posing questions and using evidence to answer them is a valuable exercise in and of itself.

Perhaps the greatest source of humility surrounds us every day. When I was a child of about ten years, I used to lie on the backyard lawn nearly every summer night, staring at the haunting mystery of the starlit sky. The Idaho town of a few hundred people in which I lived produced little light pollution, so with unaided eyes I could see the stars of Pleiades and all the brighter stars. Many of these nights under the stars I wept uncontrollably at my own insignificance compared to the vast expanse of the universe. I had never heard of Carl Sagan, but I knew I was cosmically inconsequential, dwarfed as I was by the "billions and billions of stars" above me. (Sagan did not actually use this line until publication of his last book, *Billions and Billions*. In the book, published less than two months before Sagan died, he credits late-night talk-show host Johnny Carson for using the phrase to poke fun at the cosmologist.)

These days, only rarely can I see Pleiades from my urban backyard. I almost never cry when I stare at the night sky, though my sense of awe has not lessened. Indeed, I seem to be more enamored with the majesty of the natural world with every passing year. When I'm not in the city, I need only look outside to know humility.

I am humbled that, like the millions of other species on planet Earth, we find ourselves in the magnificent position of occupying the only planet in the universe known to support life. My humility grows deeper when I realize that we have no idea how many species share the globe with us, not even within an order of magnitude. I marvel at the beauty, wonder, and complexity of each one of these species. Then I marvel at our power as we single-handedly drive half the species with which we share the planet—God's creation, as it were—to extinction by century's end.

That we have this power is truly awesome. That we use it to exterminate the species with which we share the world is the height of hubris.

These days, I rarely cry when I gaze upward at night. But I often weep when I realize how badly we are misusing our power.

Life, in its myriad forms, is almost certainly the greatest wonder in the universe. In the universe, as far as we know, life is restricted to planet Earth. Arguably, the other great wonder of the universe is the human mind, that complex product of natural selection that allows us to ask who we are, how we came to be, and why we are here. It's the mind, in other words, that inspires sufficient awe to bring us to tears in the face of nature's grandeur.

VIII

I apologize for any embarrassment I caused in my last letter. It seems I am becoming more emotional, and more willing to share my emotions, as I age. On the other hand, sentimentality is relatively new for me, if the instructor of my College Teaching class is to be believed. He met with each member of the class, outside of class, after we completed the Meyers-Briggs Type Indicator, a test that evaluates learning styles (among other attributes). In my case, he sorted through the stack of results after I identified myself, took a deep breath, looked me straight in the eye, and asked, "Have you ever shed a tear of sentiment?"

I laughed nervously, indicated that I hadn't done so very often, and he said, "No, I mean ever?" I'm pretty sure he believed me to be a sociopath. Maybe he was right. Who am I to evaluate the normalcy of others, much less myself?

A scant two decades later, my appreciation for the natural world is difficult to conceal, and, in most cases, I have lost interest in trying. That this causes discomfort is understandable, given the long history in our culture of expanding the distance between individuals and nature. William Torrey Harris, commissioner of education in the United States between 1889 and 1906, expressed and reinforced the long-standing approach in an early issue of *The Philosophy of Education*: "The great purpose of school . . . is to master the physical self, to transcend the beauty of nature. School should develop the power to withdraw from the natural world."

Harris would be ecstatic to see how far we have come. A century after Harris articulated the purpose of the educational system, Arthur Evans dedicated a chapter to education in his book, *Witchcraft and the Gay Counterculture*. I rarely agree with this author, famous for his postmodern drivel *Critique of Patriarchal Reason*, but his view on the American education system is worth repeating: "Modern schools and universities push students into habits of depersonalized learning, alienation from nature and sexuality, obedience to hierarchy, fear of authority, self-objectification, and chilling competitiveness. These character traits are the essence of the twisted personality-type of modern industrialism. They are precisely the character traits needed to maintain a social system that is utterly out of touch with nature, sexuality, and real human needs." Ecologists Paul Ehrlich and Anne Ehrlich aptly described the American social system as "capitalism for the poor, socialism for the rich," in their recent book, *One with Ninevah*. I've long found myself at odds with this system, which explains in part the discomfort I cause others (and occasionally even myself) when my emotions float to the surface.

On the other hand, I suspect that my appreciation for the natural world, which is contrary to the "great purpose of school" and maintenance of our "social system," translates into enthusiasm for the subjects I teach. Further, I am convinced students are able to recognize and appreciate enthusiasm from the first day of class. This enthusiasm facilitates our ability to reach them and teach them. Indeed, study after study and book after book routinely report that enthusiasm is the single most important element of good teaching. Of course, great teachers know their subject and are well prepared when they step into the classroom, laboratory, or field. But they also have an exceptional interest in the subject that, regardless of the teacher's age, burns passionately enough to spread sparks of interest throughout a classroom of otherwise disinterested non-majors. These are the teachers for whom students express awe years later, largely because similar zeal burns in so few bellies. Such enthusiasm probably is necessary, but not sufficient, to engender learning in the majority of students.

I do not recall when my passion for learning took root, though I do remember spending countless hours at the local library in my small hometown. Based on the few volumes in the three-room library, I assumed I would read all the books. And not merely the books in those three rooms: Lacking evidence to the contrary, I assumed I would read all published works. After all, I read a lot more than my young friends, in part because my parents encouraged my reading habit, whereas most of my friends received no such support. I first visited a significant library as a teenager, when a trip to the stacks of my future alma mater's library dashed my hopes of reading all published works. I still feel the disappointment of crushed idealism when a particularly melancholy mood is supplemented by the distinct odor of old books. Nonetheless, my teenage disappointment quickly gave way to renewed curiosity and hence enthusiasm for life's marvels. Who writes all these books? What do they have to say? I began asking these questions on the heels of my disappointing journey to a university library, and I continue to ask them.

Pursuing knowledge for its own sake is a noble enterprise, one we should encourage in students. The constant quest for context is a trait of lifelong learners. How does a new piece of knowledge fit my intellectual map of the universe? What does it reveal about past, present, and future cultures? Does it facilitate broad knowledge or deep understanding of issues important to society? These are the types of questions provoked by scholarship, and they spark my enthusiasm for teaching with every turn of the journal page and each conversation with an informed colleague.

In a chilling criticism of the pursuit of knowledge, John Keats lamented the Newtonian deconstruction of the rainbow in part II of *Lamia*. Specifically, Keats claimed that science (which was then appropriately synonymous with philosophy) robs us of the beauty of a rainbow by explaining how a prism separates light:

> "Philosophy will clip an Angel's wings,
> Conquer all mysteries by rule and line,
> Empty the haunted air, and gnomed mine—
> Unweave a rainbow."

Oxford's evolutionary biologist Richard Dawkins exposes the serious flaw in Keats' argument. In his appropriately titled book, *Unweaving the Rainbow*, Dawkins points out that those who understand the inner workings of some part of the universe are most likely to appreciate that part of the universe. An example from my own experience illustrates the point.

A few years ago, several of the graduate students with whom I am privileged to work gave me a pair of tickets for my birthday. The event was a concert by the superb contemporary pianist, George Winston. On this occasion, Winston concentrated on soft, slow pieces of extraordinary beauty. As I spasmodically jerked awake during the midst of one of Winston's wonderful songs, it occurred to me that Dawkins was exactly correct. Had I even the most rudimentary understanding of music—were I able to distinguish tones as well as the people around me—I would have been on the edge of my seat, along with most of the other patrons in the audience. Those who understand a phenomenon are most likely, not least likely, to truly appreciate its wonder and beauty. Conservation biologists, for example, are the loudest advocates for retaining the world's tremendous diversity of life, and the saddest members of society when a species is driven to extinction. We understand all too well what is lost when a species blinks out, never to be seen again.

If you're not enthusiastic, you're in the wrong business. If you're smart enough and persistent enough to make it this far in the academy, you're capable of succeeding in many fields. So, if you lack enthusiasm for the subject matter and lifelong learning, I implore you to select a field less important than academe. Perhaps I am overstating the importance of the academy, but I think not. We have in our grasps something as important as life itself: the examined life, the life of thoughtful reflection, the life of the mind. Such a life necessarily drags along with it the shrewdly logical life of the brain, the wonderfully irrational life of the heart, and the power to distinguish the difference.

IX

We've discussed several elements of teaching and learning, to the extent possible in a format that sacrifices interactivity for thoughtful reflection. This letter is particularly personal, and I think it goes straight to the heart of the educational matter. It speaks to integrity.

You can expect numerous assaults on your defenses. In my first year of teaching at a large university, a coach on the track and field team threatened me for failing to give a passing grade to an athlete who rarely managed to make it to class, even for examinations. And I was propositioned by a gorgeous young woman who said she "would do anything" to have her grade changed from a B to an A. These cases were easy to deal with, simply by ignoring them, and they are only peripherally related to the type of integrity I bring to your attention in this letter.

I am not thinking about integrity as encompassed by such terms as honesty, truthfulness, veracity, and reliability. I know you well enough to know that you will abide these values and will therefore continue to respect, nay demand, the truth and its passionate pursuit. I am thinking not about the narrow version of integrity found in the dictionary, but instead about a broader account brilliantly described by the educational luminary Parker Palmer in his book *The Courage to Teach*. As one of a handful of contemporary leaders in higher education, Palmer eloquently writes and speaks about teaching with the type of integrity that comes from within, and that can be judged only by you. You might think of this as the higher-educational application of Pelonius' advice to his son Laertas in Shakespeare's *Hamlet*: "To thine own self be true." As you surely recall from *Hamlet*, this isn't merely about the truth and nothing but the truth, nor is it about the enthusiasm about which I recently wrote. This is about the courageous expression of your convictions.

I've never questioned your ability to find parsimony, to wield Occam's razor like a surgeon's scalpel as you carve superfluous tissue from intellectual bone, sinew, and muscle. Likewise, your judgment on matters of importance has been uniformly excellent. So, I do not doubt your ability to pluck the appropriate strands of fact from the ocean of dogma swirling about your discipline, and all other disciplines. But, in the spirit of Palmer and Noddings, Maslow and Dewey, Socrates and Plato, you must come up with means of weaving those threads into a coherent tapestry that your students can claim as their own. And as with your educational predecessors, the means must be unique to you. You cannot thoughtlessly pick and choose the threads of your intellectual ancestors; in attempting to do so, you might find yourself instead stuck with Parker Palmer's unfounded mysticism, Nel Noddings' misguided postmodernism, Maslow's intransigence, and Dewey's decimal system. Allow me a paragraph's worth of divergence regarding the disadvantages of Palmer, Noddings, and Maslow before I return to the subject at hand.

The First Amendment notwithstanding, we should teach the glory of evidence, rather than the spirits Palmer finds so enthralling. I tolerate and even appreciate cultures and worldviews that differ from my own, and I encourage you to do the same. But we should draw the rational line at encouraging mysticism in the science classroom. Extreme forms of postmodernism are similarly fraught with conceptual hurdles, which might explain why the enterprise deconstructed itself out of existence by the dawn of the twenty-first century; we should not backslide into an alternative universe that allows students to accept every personal view as equivalent to reality. On the other hand, we should not follow Maslow's lead in forcing a continuum of understanding into a series of discrete boxes. John Dewey's intellectual armor is not without its chinks (consider this tidbit of creativity-destroying, anti-intellectual coercive pandering from the famous industrial educator: "Every teacher should realize he is a social servant set apart for the maintenance of the proper social order and the securing of the right social growth"), but it was actually Melville Dewey who invented the book-cataloging system (I couldn't resist the shallow humor). Melville's other scholastic contributions were similarly limited, which is small wonder given that he spent much of his time getting fired for practicing Judaism. Unlike most of your educational predecessors, the past is not dead. But you should not allow the ghosts of the educational past to hold the keys to your future.

How, then, should you tap into your integrity to expose the gifted teacher within you?

Unlike most of your predecessors, you have ready access to an abundance of wonderful tools and ideas: your predecessors, for example, and words they have written. Thousands of tips, techniques, and tricks are described in myriad journals, newsletters, books, and websites, all of which apparently are poised for installation into the modern teacher's arsenal. Notable among these is the impressive variety of resources about teaching and learning offered by Jossey-Bass, the educational imprint of publishing giant Wiley. Some of my favorite techniques are found in Magna Publications' *The Teaching Professor* newsletter, and in books such as Wilbert McKeachie's *Teaching Tips*, Margaret Morganrot Gullette's *The Art and Craft of Teaching*, Kenneth Eble's *Professors as Teachers*, and Blythe and Sweet's *It Works for Me!* For early-career teachers, I recommend Peter Filene's *The Joy of Teaching* and Eble's *The Craft of Teaching* (the titles of both are imminently revealing). I encourage you to study these resources, and many others, for specific techniques. Try the ones that appeal to you, usually with modification. But be careful to avoid "becoming" the techniques, to losing yourself in the styles of others. After all, you should rely on the techniques only until your inner teacher arrives on the scene.

As you sample the wide variety of teaching techniques at your disposal, you'll discover and co-opt the ones that work for you. Thus, you will ultimately use only the specific techniques that become part of your teaching persona. Some classroom strategies perfectly fit your wit and sense of irony, whereas others do not. For example, the use of humor described in Ronald Berk's *Professors Are from*

Mars, Students Are from Snickers is generally too farcically vaudevillian for your dry wit, nourished as it is by your profound sense of irony. Your firm grasp of literature will serve you well in any course; your disregard for popular culture, which I share, suggests that you should not use contemporary television programming as a starting point for classroom discussion.

I hope you continue to study and implement techniques throughout your career; life is a journey, after all, and this is particularly true of a teacher's life. Some of the techniques will fit poorly and you will discard them after an attempt or two. Others will strike a chord with you and your class and you'll keep them in the toolkit for years to come. Still others will evolve with you until they become unrecognizable from the original source and inseparable from your classroom persona. When the techniques support your integrity and passion, you'll know you've arrived: You are teaching from the heart, true to yourself.

Revel in this sense of harmony between you, your students, and the subject matter, but do not become complacent about it. If fame is atypical and fleeting, harmony in the classroom is even more rare and transient. Achieving "the zone" in which your classroom pulses with the energy of inquiry and teachable moments bubble up like sparkling water from an artesian well is a seductive and ephemeral experience. Cherish this sensation and hope you can remember it long after the moment fades. You might use the same techniques to teach the same material to a different group of students an hour after achieving educational nirvana, only to find that the fog of indifference has settled over the energy of inquiry like a damp blanket, thereby obscuring the teachable moments that appeared on cue such a short time ago. Fumbling awkwardly through a valley of ignorant lethargy, you'll wonder how Sisyphus found the energy to keep pushing that rock up the hill. In his case, the gods, who undoubtedly would have done worse to him if he'd stopped, dictated the punishment. Likewise, I suppose, during these times, we might be well advised to remember that worse punishments await us outside academe.

My hope for you is that your integrity and passion impel your constant pursuit of educational peaks. I hope that teachable moments arrive in perfect synchrony with the notes in your hand and the thoughts in your head, that your quest for educational nirvana is fulfilled early and often, and that you take time to revel in the glow when the blissful feeling arrives.

X

Everything is connected to everything else, although some connections are more tenuous and less clear than others. Sometimes when you pull a rogue thread from your sweater, you get the thread; other times, the whole sweater unravels. You should help students recognize that (a) some connections are vitally important (they'll loosen the tangled knot, thus salvaging the sweater), and (b) they need to develop the skills to determine which ones are vital. Some systems crucially depend on all the pieces—all the threads, as it were—or they will fail to function normally. Others depend on a foundational sense on critical elements.

Critical thinking forms the foundation for recognizing which elements underpin an informed and introspective life. Communication allows learned discourse with others. As such, the abilities to think critically and communicate well are fundamental to a full life. Critical thinkers who become articulate speakers and writers are well on their way to a life of considerable success and satisfaction. Given the state of popular culture in America, plenty of material presents itself for critique. Even our bumper stickers are rich sources for social criticism.

"Support the Troops," pleads the back of seemingly half the cars in America. And no wonder: We're almost always engaged in wars we initiate, a trend that is likely to maintain itself as we continue to elect war-mongers to our highest public offices.

Despite the lack of commitment demonstrated by the use of transient magnets instead of more permanent stickers, who wouldn't support the troops? Unless, of course, doing so required some sort of minor sacrifice on behalf of the person driving the SUV sporting the magnet.

"Pray the Rosary," seems innocuous enough. I suppose doing so is no more harmful than wishing upon a star or placing one's faith in a unicorn on the dark side of the moon. But I've never seen a bumper sticker suggesting I take either of those actions.

"Grow the Economy." I'll admit I've never seen this bumper sticker. There is no need for it because the idea is not contentious or political. Elected government officials, advertising campaigns, religious groups, and the media all implore us to spend beyond our means, even though doing so will result in the collapse of our so-called civilization. Better sooner than later, I suppose, if we're interested in saving cultures and non-human species.

All teachers should underscore the importance of critical thinking and articulate communication, though I recognize that most of us will be rewarded rarely or not at all for promoting these heretical ideas. The rare reward invariably comes in the form of a student's comment, often several years after the student has departed. Before I describe how I attempt to instill critical thinking and communication skills, indulge me a couple of specific examples, one each from the arenas of thinking and writing.

I came across John at a professional meeting a year after he completed a course with me. A lifetime scholar with a full-time job off campus, John is a decade older than the usual incoming student, which might explain why he was always quietly thoughtful in the classroom. He didn't say much off campus, either, the few times I encountered him. He clearly preferred listening to talking, an approach so seldom employed in this day and age that it seems quaintly old-fashioned. After a few minutes of small talk, John steered the conversation toward the class he'd taken a year earlier.

John mentioned that he was "taken aback" by the class. My quizzical expression prodded him to elaborate. Apparently, I kept asking what the students thought, kept probing, forcing them to think and articulate their thoughts. I didn't just "feed" them the answers, and then ask them to spit them back out for the exams. John admitted that this was new to him, that he couldn't figure out what I was doing, much less why. He went on to say that almost nobody teaches this way, and that it took a few class periods to become accustomed to the approach. He mentioned the discomfort in actually thinking deeply instead of writing furiously. Somewhat taken aback myself, I asked John if he disliked the approach. He said he thought it was refreshing, unusual, difficult, but ultimately worthwhile because be became more comfortable "thinking on his feet." He also admitted that he spends time each day just reflecting on what he's heard, what he's read, and what he should do next, in his job and his life.

This is a minor example, almost trivial. Perhaps John was merely filling conversational space in a complimentary manner. Whether he was or not, I suspect there is at least a grain of truth to his commentary on the virtual absence of critical reflection in the classroom. If so, we should dedicate considerable effort to overcoming this problem. If John's experience is representative, our efforts could be rewarded with the development of a critically reflective citizenry. This outcome clearly has positive implications for all humanity.

At times, I've more faith in the unsolicited, unexpected, but closely examined comment than in the one forced by an unplanned encounter. On a particularly gray, overcast afternoon, I had come home early in an attempt to recover from a minor virus that was revealing itself a few days after a cross-country trip on a commercial airline. Though clearly not life-threatening, this particular bug was hampering my productivity and darkening my mood.

I was escaping the stack of papers that demanded grades by descending into a well-deserved afternoon nap. The telephone rudely interrupted and I could not resist the urge to answer it. My wife is superior in this regard (and to be truthful, most others): She is quite capable of screening calls via the answering machine. But my obsessive-compulsive personality will not allow two rings, much less the requisite four before the machine takes over. After all, there was a slim chance the caller was a student in need. I insist to students that their education is more important than my sleep, and I therefore encourage them to call me at home, day or night. Nonetheless, I doubt many students expected to catch me napping at home shortly after class on a weekday afternoon.

I recall groaning a half-hearted "hello," surprised I could not muster a more positive tone. On the other hand, I fully expected a solicitor to insist upon cleaning the carpets in my carpet-free house.

The voice coming through the receiver seemed familiar, but immediate recognition eluded me. I implored my mind to work faster, but the synapses failed to fire. The pause revealed my ignorance, and Emma finally identified herself.

Emma had graduated from our program four years previously. She returned to school after a ten-year career in the fast-paced world of private consulting, where she was resoundingly successful by all contemporary American measures. But she was not completely satisfied with her high-paying corporate job, so she wanted to obtain a degree that would better enable her to "save the world." She was a model student in my upper-division course, and I had subsequently served on her graduate advisory committee. Such service had allowed me to review several drafts of her dissertation. A public servant in a federal land-management agency, Emma periodically seeks advice about technical matters.

In this case, Emma had called just to thank me. She even admitted that few students appreciate the time teachers spend trying to improve a student's writing. I recall this tidbit because I remember thinking "few is an understatement." Emma was calling to express her thanks because her co-workers routinely commented on her excellent writing skills. She had received accolades from her supervisor and even from the public for preparing an environmental assessment of a complex, contentious issue. She read several of the favorable comments submitted by private citizens, and concluded, "There is a lot of *you* in my writing."

We chatted for a few minutes, and then said our goodbyes. Invigorated in body and spirit, I felt more certain than ever that grading could be meaningful. My nap, so near a few minutes previously, was now out of the question: Those papers could wait no longer.

When taken seriously, grading is painful for you and your students. But learning is a painful process, and it's only fair that teachers share a small part of the pain. Other than grading papers with care and diligence, a topic about which I wrote at length previously, how can you promote excellence in thinking, speaking, and writing?

First and foremost, insist on evidence. Emotion is wonderful, and you should use all the emotions at your disposal to teach and learn. Allow your anger, your serenity, your passion, and your devotion to fuel your pursuit of knowledge and its transmission. Harness these emotions, but do not allow them to capture you, to derail you from objectively evaluating evidence. Read Nel Noddings' *Educating for Intelligent Belief or Unbelief* and use it as one basis for discussing epistemology. How do we know what we claim to know? How do we distinguish the infinite wonder of reality from the sterile (but allegedly wondrous) promise of mysticism? Read (and question) everything you can by the evolutionary biologist Richard Dawkins, and apply his rigorous standards of logic to every classroom discussion. Among Dawkins' writings is a letter to his ten-year-old daughter in which he implores her to use evidence as a basis for her beliefs instead of the far more popular bases of authority, tradition, and revelation. Question authority until you understand the mechanism by which the world works, and insist your students do the same. In a similar vein, question tradition as a basis for your actions and those of your students.

Nearly all people belong to the religion of their parents, and they believe what they've been told to believe. There is no evidentiary basis for many of their beliefs, and some of them defy reason altogether. You will have great difficulty convincing your students that their beliefs are "wrong." But if you can convince them to use evidence instead of tradition or authority, you will leave them better prepared for an examined life than you found them. Finally, discard revelation as a basis for knowledge. Religious leaders and national-level Republican politicians commonly rely on revelation for "knowledge," and they exploit their positions of authority to pass along this "knowledge" from one generation to the next. But in the absence of evidence, revelation, authority, and tradition are invalid reasons for believing anything. If you teach only one thing in every course you offer, let it be evaluation of various reasons for believing.

I have already mentioned Socratic dialogue as one important technique to inspire thoughtful responses. A significant body of research indicates that students learn and retain information when they think about it, instead of merely transferring notes from your pages to theirs. But you'll need to give them time to formulate a response, and this is no small task. Because you will have thought about the topic before showing up for class, you'll have an answer in mind (and perhaps on the pages in front of you). As such, letting the question hang on the air for thirty seconds will seem a lifetime for you, if not for everybody else in the classroom. Even the best-prepared students will need time to absorb the question, place it into context, and formulate a reasoned response. And the students from whom you do not solicit a response still need time to listen and think. Obviously, the questions must be interesting: If they are too slight or too weighty, students will disengage from the dialogue.

Socrates was onto something, but he was working with small groups of scholars. Perhaps you'll have the luxury of working with small classes most of the time. But do not forsake the challenge and opportunity of working with large classes, which will test your skills and allow you to reach the masses. If your message is important, it should reach hundreds of people each year, instead of a few dozen; if it's not important, why waste precious time with it? Perhaps the best way to capture the interest of students in large classes is to make the classes seem small.

Many techniques are designed specifically to increase the intimacy of large classes. I prefer techniques that commence with student–student interactions and then shift to a discussion that engages the entire class. Write-pair-share exercises are ideal in this regard. These exercises begin with a question or statement to which students can respond. The question or statement should adhere to the Goldilocks canon, being neither too slight nor too weighty. Students then take a few moments to think about, and write about, the topic. Writing forces the brain to engage with the subject and to express the resulting thoughts in an articulate manner, as well as providing a set of notes for future reference. Depending on the complexity of the question, you'll want to allow students to think and write for thirty seconds to two minutes: Less time will not allow them to reflect and record, and more time suggests the question is too complex for this exercise. The idea is to engage them, not lose them to their own writing. After they've had time to think and record ideas, students "pair up" with their neighbors to share ideas in an informal and nonthreatening environment. After a minute or two, solicit a few responses from the classroom, emphasizing that an idea should not be offered with "authorship" attached: There is no need to indicate whether the idea came from the student presenting the idea, the person she "paired" with, or the interaction between her and her partner. Thus, the group can focus on ideas, not the people with which they originated. Such an approach is not only relatively unintimidating, it represents a noble model for lifelong scholarship.

The write-pair-share exercise can be modified in myriad ways to meet your purposes and introduce variety into your classroom. You can use "think-pair-share," forgoing writing for critical reflection. After writing or thinking, students can discuss their ideas in groups of two, then four, so that they can fully develop their ideas before presenting them to a large group. The small-group discussion can be comprised of any reasonable number of students, including zero (i.e., you can proceed directly from thinking and writing to a large-group sharing of ideas). This exercise can be used to produce a simple list of facts (e.g., "Who is your favorite Shakespearean character?") or to generate hypotheses (e.g., "Why do people lie?"). The former list could serve as a starting point for analyzing the creation and development of characters (e.g., for classes in literature or creative writing) or debilitating character flaws (psychology, sociology, political science), whereas the latter could provide the basis for discussing human behavior (criminal justice, psychology, child development, education, behavioral ecology). If you pay attention to the development of your in-class exercises, students will try to "fit" their responses into the framework of the resulting lecture or discussion, and therefore will be engaged to a greater extent than if you simply provide and describe a list in which you think they should be interested.

This family of techniques encourages thoughtful reflection and articulation of ideas in written and spoken forms. It provides feedback in a nonconfrontational manner by allowing students to evaluate their responses in light of the lecture or discussion following the exercise. And it gives you an opportunity to "shrink" a large class into groups small enough to efficiently and effectively support reflection, interaction, communication, and feedback. You can employ many other specific techniques in your classes, regardless of class size and subject. I encourage you to seek and use them if they seem capable of engendering skills in critical thinking, public speaking, and informed writing. Interaction with peers and feedback (from peers and teachers) are desirable goals to the extent they facilitate development of these crucial skills.

Lest I be misunderstood, I am not suggesting we employ strategies to "shrink" class sizes in a political vacuum. Rather, I strongly encourage you to work toward the small classes in which we know learning is accelerated. Reducing the size of classes requires a political commitment to education that is largely lacking from our society, and "active learning" strategies incorrectly give the impression that professors can overcome society's lack of commitment to turn out informed, enlightened students from classes with a thousand students. But these techniques represent triage in a crisis, not solutions to systemic problems.

As I have indicated previously, techniques, such as write-pair-share, are great until the teacher arrives. But technique without content, just like content without a delivery system, is insufficient. *What* to teach is crucial, of course, and I have a few thoughts on this topic. If you like, I will share them in a future letter.

XI

Thank you for your recent letter, which reminds me of the supreme importance of how we teach. *How* we teach is more important than *what* we teach, as suggested by our rich series of letters on the former topic. But you've nearly exhausted me, and my knowledge of classroom mechanics. This, then, will be my last comment about how to teach. In many ways, it contains the most valuable advice I can offer.

Your class might be the most important thing in your life. At the very least, it's near the top of your list of essential activities. After all, your primary responsibility for the academic term is the few classes you are teaching during any particular semester. You've already agreed that you are passionate about what you teach, and that teaching gives you the opportunity to share your passion with others. And let's face it, that list of essential activities is hardly brimming. Unless you are the rare individual faced with a life-threatening malady, you're pretty comfortable with your lot in life.

By the time you find yourself ensconced in the classroom, your finances don't pose much of a challenge. You're making a living wage, and—unless you're an exceptional American—spending slightly more than you're earning. You've got a comfortable place to live. More importantly, you've likely settled issues of the heart, and of the soul. You've got a partner or you're happy to be without one. If you've got one, you've already decided on the number and timing of your children. Religion, or the absence of it, no longer troubles you as it once did. As much as you'd like to think otherwise, you've settled in.

Contrast your life with that of your typical student. She may be uncertain of her sexuality; if she's not, she's probably uncertain about when and with whom to have sex. American culture has convinced her that she should be seriously looking for a long-term partner, so she spends much of her time in party mode, preparing for it, or recovering from it. Her evolutionarily derived maternal instincts, reinforced by culture, constantly nag at her psyche. Her friends are getting married (but not yet divorced). Her parents are talking about splitting up, and her grandmother teeters at the edge of death (a death that will come, of course, the day before the midterm exam). Peppered with arguments rooted in reason, she seriously questions her spirituality, perhaps for the first time. The bombardment of hormones, peer pressure, and general busy-ness has her contemplating suicide on a regular basis. Do you still think your class is the most important activity in her life? Remember, it's one of a handful of courses that she struggles to keep up with as she sorts through the important issues in her life. And unlike you, she hasn't settled on a vocation yet, so she has no idea if your class is remotely related to her career. Her best day is filled with myriad issues and events more important than your class. On her worst days—and she probably has many of them each term—your class does not enter her mind. Yes, she's got a severe case of Center of the Universe Syndrome (C.U.S.). At least she's got a legitimate excuse, unlike our many colleagues who suffer from the same affliction. You should be thankful she comes to your class on her good days, much less her bad ones.

It's been said that the best indication of a man's character is how he treats those who can do nothing for him. Although their fragile egos do not allow them to let it show, your students are delicate human beings with little or no control over your life. If you choose, you can influence their lives. Your influence can be positive or negative, or you might choose to create distance between you and your students. The latter approach makes you largely invisible, thus protecting you from potential embarrassment and perhaps even from the occasional legal challenge.

I often read or hear this bit of advice, and I'm sure you do, too. The standard line is to maintain an appropriate professional distance from your students. Don't spend time and energy getting to know them. And—horror of horrors—don't ever touch one of them. They'll only let you down or worse: They'll sue you. Furthermore, the pedigreed professor must command respect from each of her lowly students. You can't command respect if your humanity is hanging out for all to see.

This much-repeated bit of nonsense comes from the cover-your-ass (CYA) handbook lovingly drafted by the legal aides who work for your institution's administrators. This gang can evaluate neither teaching nor learning, but they can adeptly quantify bricks and mortar, publications, and grant funds. The CYA advice is misguided for at least four reasons. Please let me know if you think of others;

as you know, I am constantly searching for arguments to throw at the typically visionless administrator. Not because it does any good in the short term, but because I relish the satisfaction of pointing out the idiocy of most administrators and because doing so makes them feel good about keeping my salary unjustifiably low. It seems selfish to deny them this simple pleasure.

First, your students will not care about you—and by extension the subject you are trying to teach—unless they know that you care. Specifically, they need to know that you care about them. Not all of them, of course: Every class contains a few unfeeling automatons who might turn into fine clerks or college administrators some day. But most of your students have hopes and dreams, and they are enrolled in your class because they want you to help them realize their aspirations. They certainly aren't taking my class—and they better not be taking yours—because it's an easy A for the transcript. You cannot possibly help the typical student realize his dream unless you can pick it out of a lineup. That applies to the dream as well as the student.

Second, creating distance between you and your students does not guarantee their respect for you. At its best, this type of "respect" merely causes students to forget about you and the subject matter as soon as class is finished. At its worst, this is the type of "respect" prisoners have for guards. It's a rare guard who is treated with respect when the prisoners gain control of the prison. Reasonably intelligent students will see through the charade of artificial distance, thus causing it to backfire. As a result of differences in age, life experiences, and degrees, there is already plenty of distance between you and the students you are trying to reach. If you want to educate them, you should try to break down the barriers. If you're successful, you can engender some genuine respect that enhances long-term learning.

Many of my colleagues talk about the "line" between them and their students. In their view, neither first-year students nor late-career Ph.D. students may cross this "line" of deference. For these colleagues, students who cross this imaginary line do so at their own risk, albeit almost always in ignorance.

There is no line for students to cross. Are you more knowledgeable about your discipline than students? I should hope so. Does this allow you to be offended by a student who is "too familiar," thereby giving you free rein to use your esteemed position as bully pulpit? I've been fortunate enough to influence a few fine students, and they've been kind enough to let me know. I keep at this seemingly thankless job because such incidents come along now and then.

The third reason is more general. At the heart of this issue is what it means to be human. One measure of our humanity is how we treat those who differ from us: different species, different cultures, different individuals. As I've written before, we all differ from everybody else, a trait guaranteed by our unique genetic coding. Differences in DNA are reinforced by variation in life experiences. But, as should be self-evident, different does not translate to "better." Thus, you are undoubtedly more knowledgeable about your discipline than most. But, like all humans, you are ignorant about many things. The thought of any student giving you a quiz on her specialty should give you pause, until you are willing to acknowledge your ignorance beyond that specialized arena you claim as your own.

A fourth reason, perhaps the most selfish, involves the relationship between your personal and professional lives. What kind of person teaches without emotion? Many academicians are more skillful teachers than you or I. But how many teach as if their lives, and the lives of their students, mattered? Do you want to live a life without love for your job? After all, you likely will spend more time working, at least for the next few decades, than on any other activity. Can you respect yourself if you strive for the lowest level of connection with other human being? In so doing, are you not depriving yourself of a world of happiness?

Once you acknowledge, nay embrace, your ignorance, you will be able to recognize the value of knowing your students. You will appreciate the perspectives they each bring, as informed by that unique combination of DNA and life experience. In so doing, your life will be enriched as I hope you are enriching the lives of your students.

Your time on the planet is stunningly brief. During that blink of time, you will interact with far too few people who care about the issues you find utterly enthralling. Why would you treat those few people with the disrespect commonly set aside for "lower" forms of life? Should we not embrace them as fellow pioneers on our quest for a just and sustainable human civilization? Are we not all on the same journey, thirsting for the same knowledge? Thoreau's guidance on this point is useful. In *The*

Maine Woods, he insisted that those who "would learn the secrets of nature" would be forced to "practice more humanity than others."

Students are humans, and so am I. It only seems natural that I have grown to dislike some of the students I have taught, just as it seems natural that I have grown to love some of them. Civility demands tolerance for those I dislike. Humanity requires expressing my feelings to those I love.

I hasten to add that this is not lust (though I've known, and to the best of my ability, concealed that feeling about many a student). And it is not the same version of love I feel for my wife, parents, siblings, or even in-laws, whom I must appreciate, if for no other reason than for bringing my wife into the world and raising her to be the warm, wise woman she is. But it is an emotional commitment that runs far beyond the feelings I have for my mechanic or the owner of my favorite restaurant.

And why should we expect otherwise? These students have matured before my eyes. With many of them, I've spent countless hours in the laboratory and field. We've collected ecological data for twelve hours under the blazing sun in the Arizona desert, shared a meal and a story, and then slept under a shared roof before rising early to do it over again. We've diligently pored over the data we've collected, found the story buried in the data, and journeyed to marginally exotic locales to discuss it with other scholars. I've lived vicariously through my students: soared with them as they fell in love, despaired with them when they fell back out, struggled to help them recover from the death of a loved one, even mourned with them as one of their peers tragically, suddenly died in the prime of his young life. I reserve my most bitter laugh for colleagues who tell me there is a "line" the student should not cross.

Taking my advice seriously could place your career at risk. Better your career than your humanity.

XII

Teach the courses you are assigned, and no others. Taking such a minimalist approach will keep you plenty busy, if you teach with conviction. Try as I might, I cannot seem to make teaching anything less than an all-consuming activity even during a semester marked by only one graduate seminar. Perhaps I am a slow learner (many of my former instructors can vouch for this) and an inefficient instructor (I suspect many of my current students will vouch for this), but keeping up with even a single course is a full-time job. In addition to learning the hopes and dreams of each student, there are the never-ending tasks of developing meaningful assignments, grading them fairly and with compassion, availing myself to each student, reviewing current events and connecting them to classroom activities and student's lives, reading about pedagogical theory and practice, and myriad other items, large and small.

In the face of these tasks, which I view as necessities, I struggle mightily to meet the constant demand for new scholarship, community outreach, professional service, and maintenance of fragile relationships with colleagues. It seems most of these are necessities, not luxuries. Paying them proper attention challenges my ability to row my little dinghy, not to mention keep it from sinking beneath the heavy seas of the generating scholarship, conducting service activities, and maintaining my own social network. And I fear the wake of fast-moving intellectual yachts maneuvered by my colleagues will engulf our students, many of who are bobbing hopefully in their leaky life rafts. Something simply has to give, and we shouldn't let the "something" be the students. I would rather steal a page from the Buddha's playbook than drown students in a sea of intellectual competition. The Buddha made quite a name for himself in the process of teaching only two things: the cause of suffering and how to end it. In other words, he taught the most rare and most important of human attributes, empathy. Of course, your courses can and should evolve over time, but there is no need to offer a new course with every fresh idea you have. And there is little to be gained from teaching new courses if you cannot give up others.

Rather than constantly adding new courses to your arsenal, teach the truly weighty concepts within the context of your requisite teaching load. Such an approach will ensure your courses are timely, substantive, and important. They will reduce the number of times a student hears the same thing from you, in the three classes of yours she completes. In all of your efforts, I encourage you to focus on skills that facilitate lifelong learning.

I realize that many topics are important within any particular discipline, especially to intellectuals who focus on little else. But I also have come to the conclusion that few themes matter more than social equity and environmental protection. As such, my courses focus on these subjects. It seems to me that these concepts fit hand-in-glove in every curriculum and nearly every course. How could English literature courses avoid matters of justice? How could chemistry, physics, and even mathematics, fail to incorporate examples of environmental protection? The curricula in which social equity and environmental protection do not fit are those I am working hard to destroy because they are marked by courses that further American-style capitalism, to the detriment of dignity and humanity. Such courses are particularly prevalent in business programs, colleges of agriculture, and many of the sciences.

The prevalence of ideas that are consistent with popular culture and also counter to the mission of higher education is one manifestation of a disturbing trend toward technological solutions and enterprises at the expense of deep thinking and lifelong learning. Institutions of higher education increasingly reflect cultural norms in their laser-like focus on acquisition of financial wealth, even at the expense of an examined, rewarding life. (I am not suggesting that an examined life is necessarily worth living; Socrates famously commented on the unexamined life but, as nearly as I can tell, he passed no corresponding judgment on the examined life. Indeed, a couple of millennia after Socrates said the unexamined life was not worth living, Schopenhauer pointed out that the examined life is worse!). This theme is consistent with the acquisition of skills sufficient to obtain a high-paying job instead of those needed to become intellectually, emotionally, and physically self-sufficient.

Colleges and universities provide positive reinforcement for the notion that they are designed to supply corporate America with the bodies and brains to enable success (of the corporations, not the individuals serving them). Institutions of higher education have joined government as pawns of industry, as reflected in the lifelong pursuits of most Americans. Our citizenry is willing to tolerate high school only because it is necessary for college. High-school graduates tolerate higher education because it underlies the desired "good job" waiting in the "real world." Life in the work place is tolerated only because retirement looms. Thus, life is comprised of a series of wretched trials to be impatiently endured while genuine reward lurks around the next corner. But we recognize the importance of lifelong learning, and perhaps the inextricably intertwined lifelong living, when we inspiringly refer to graduation as "commencement." Graduation marks a beginning, not an end. Or, in the words of John Dewey: "Education is not preparation of life; education is life itself."

If the blind pursuit of wealth on behalf of American industry is the contemporary version of living well, I'd rather not. Doing so seems to be the Earthly equivalent of forgoing terrestrial pleasure on behalf of a promised (but undelivered and undeliverable) heavenly reward. Folk singer Jimmy Buffet expressed this as dying while living, as opposed to living while dead. (I beg you to ignore his trivial songs about cheeseburgers while I attempt to make a minor point.) Nobody gets out alive: Better to make a difference for future generations than to live as if they don't matter.

I implore you to help stop this race to the bottom of the capitalist junk heap. We must restore our focus on education for the sake of knowing, reflecting, understanding, and empathizing. This might require us, as individuals and institutions, to steer away from the fool's gold of financial "security" so readily marketed by the corporations that have come to dominate our culture.

XIII

As I suggested in my last missive, your career is far too short to spend on irrelevant minutia. You should teach the courses you are required to teach, and focus them on matters of import. If everything you teach contributes to development of a just, sustainable human society, you're doing fine. If not, I encourage you to reconsider the topics you have chosen. Fortunately, this arena is large enough to accommodate each discipline and every learner. Unfortunately, as I have indicated previously, this route requires you to swim upstream against a substantial current.

Societal relevance is a fine place to start. It wasn't long ago that institutions of higher education pursued scholarship that was potentially significant to society and its citizens, a tradition that began with Socrates and Plato. Consider, for example, rapid advances in medicine and its application after World War II, environmental protection and rehabilitation throughout the 1970s and 1980s, and renewable energy technologies during the last quarter-century. These examples belie a shift in higher education away from sustainability and justice for underrepresented groups, a shift that clearly reflects the increasingly entrenched neo-conservatism of the United States.

A few words from Thomas Jefferson provide a glimmer of hope regarding national-level politics. In a letter to John Taylor in June of 1798, Jefferson wrote a few prescient words shortly after passage of the Sedition Act and before his barely successful run for the presidency: "A little patience, and we shall see the reign of witches pass over, their spells dissolve, and the people, recovering their true sight, restore their government to it's true principles. It is true that in the mean time we are suffering deeply in spirit, and incurring the horrors of war & long oppressions of enormous public debt. . . . If the game runs sometimes against us at home we must have patience till luck turns, & then we shall have an opportunity of winning back the principles we have lost, for this is a game where principles are at stake."

A few principled institutions still hold themselves accountable to society, despite the absence of incentives for universities and the faculty that comprise them. Inspiration can be found, for example, at Portland, Oregon's Lewis and Clark College, which recently became the country's first institution of higher education to hold itself to the standards of the Kyoto Protocol on greenhouse gas emissions. It's a small step, to be sure, but positive examples are so few that even such token efforts as this one are inspiring. But the big money, and therefore the majority of scholarship, is found in the dismantling of environmental protections and exploitation of the underprivileged. Seldom are public colleges or their employees rewarded, financially or otherwise, for conducting scholarship or teaching courses focused on environmental protection or social justice. After all, we obtain too few of our funds from taxpayers, and therefore have to rely on the deep pockets of large corporations to support research and, especially tragically, teaching.

As I have written in a recent book, American-style capitalism can be viewed as the pinnacle of mass murder. Consider the resource-extractive industries that produce much of the world's pollution while impeding social justice (large oil and mining companies top the list, but American-style capitalism rewards the many corporations that follow their leads). These are the companies that destroy native cultures and species for the sake of financial gain (though to be fair, they wouldn't be capable of these egregious transgressions without considerable support from the multitude of conspicuous consumers in American society). Because they have the cash, these companies fund big-money research, the results of which further ensure their continued financial dominance on the global stage. Like hounds on the trail of chubby, dawdling rabbits, colleges and universities chase these companies in hot pursuit of gold. The incessant siren of commerce drowns out the occasional squawk of a sacrificial golden goose. Collateral damage is widely accepted in the bloody battle for short-term financial security.

The academy's fading interest in societal relevance is bearing the expectedly rotten fruit. The decline in public support for institutions of higher education directly reflects the disdain with which these institutions have held public opinion. I am an avid supporter of esoteric research, and it is obvious to me that the most theoretical of research programs have borne exceptionally rich rewards for society. I'm a big fan of the famous toast at Cambridge University: "To pure mathematics. May it never be of any practical use whatsoever." But the academy has simply ignored its potential supporters in society, rarely making any effort to demonstrate the dividends of esoteric scholarship to the citizenry. The serious scholar seems to believe that public lectures, articles in popular press, and media interviews are beneath him, and his institution's administrators promote this view by rewarding only the accomplishments that are easily counted. Buildings, grant funds, and refereed publications are rewarded while transformative educational experiences and multidisciplinary faculty governance are paid the obligatory lip service, albeit in an infrequent whisper. It is small surprise, then, that the citizenry has little understanding of higher education's self-constructed ivory tower and even less interest in paying the electric bill to run its elevators, despite the fact that an increasing proportion of them are sending their children to college in the hope their kids will achieve gainful employment, if not a well-rounded education.

No quick fix will bring together the academy and the citizens they serve. The erosion of societal support can be restored, but only if academicians are willing to reach out to the masses for many years to come. These informal efforts must match our classroom endeavors in their attention to topics of import. I propose a few examples in the paragraphs that follow, although I suspect you can generate a superior list.

My first example is so nationalistic you might accuse me of hyperpatriotism, and I would be hard-pressed to defend myself against the charge. I am thinking of this country's impending collapse. There seems little question that the neo-conservative agenda is accelerating our financial insolvency and therefore the demise of the American Empire. History indicates that every empire dissolves eventually, and substantial empires typically collapse a generation or two after they reach their zenith. The United States is the most unsustainable civilization in the history of the world, and we've no reason to believe we will persist when so many other empires have failed.

Lacking a crystal ball, I cannot predict how the country will collapse. Perhaps the neo-conservative pursuit of terrorists will cause financial insolvency, and we'll simply follow the Soviet Union's lead in declaring bankruptcy (though it would be unwise to give Osama bin Laden too much credit for bringing the U.S.S.R.—or the U.S.A.—to its knees). Or perhaps at some point the rapidly increasing proportion of our citizens living in poverty will realize the source of their suffering and will cease to tolerate, much less support, contemporary neo-conservative policies and those who create them. If history provides clues, the demise of the American Empire will result from several factors working subtly in concert. Perhaps I will be surprised, and we will merely lose influence without collapsing beneath the weight of our own hubris; perhaps our fall will resemble that of Great Britain, rather than of Easter Island. I suspect most Americans would prefer the former to the latter.

Of course, I feel horribly sad for the teenagers and college students who will never live to see America as a benevolent republic. On the other hand, I am comforted that the unwilling sacrifices of this generation, and the next, might allow many of the world's cultures and species to survive. If our demise comes rapidly, our aggressive pursuit of material "goods" and the associated creation of pollution will inflict horrific atrocities on the world's cultures and species for another decade or two, but then we will fade to irrelevance. When that happens, we should celebrate on behalf of the world's species and cultures.

Nobody wants to fall on his sword, and I am no exception. But because we're falling anyway, we might as well enjoy the truly good news resulting from our collapse. Demise of an empire is analogous to death of an individual; both are fully expected, and both should spark celebration. Edward Abbey, the iconoclastic Southwestern writer, described this sort of *Good News* in his book with the same title.

In addition to providing a ray of hope for many of the world's occupants, we have plenty of other good news to spread in the classroom and beyond. My short list of topics worth teaching includes morality, argumentation (and its close cousin, skepticism), consilience, cooperation, communication skills, overcoming oppression, assessing one's ecological impact, and history. Much of this information will help close the gap between our institutions and the citizenry, to the benefit of both. The importance of the latter subject is self-evident: Most students have not heard of Giordano Bruno, for example. As always, I welcome your comments on this list of topics. Perhaps I have included too little, too much, or the wrong type of information.

I believe that every class, public appearance, and publication should have a moral basis. Nel Noddings is the greatest advocate for a moral education, particularly in her compelling book, *The Challenge to Care in Schools*. By many specific steps, we can teach intellectual reflection and ethical behavior. I will briefly describe only a few, leaving you to pursue others in the expansive literature on the topic.

The mother of all questions is the spiritual one. The existence of a god, or multiple gods, has vexed every human culture since we first acquired brains large enough to question deeply. In the absence of knowledge, we have invoked spirits as a band-aid to ignorance. More recently, the Abrahamic religions have invoked a single spirit, as opposed to multiple deities summoned by previous cultures. As a scientist, I am uncomfortable depending on ghost stories as valid explanations for the inner workings of the universe. When spiritually inclined students (which is nearly all of them) inquire about my religious beliefs, I tell them I simply believe in one less god than do most Americans. And I suggest that when we finally admit that we are alone on this rock, we can summon the courage to begin treating each other with respect, valuing each other and our own dignity. Heaven and hell, if they exist, are found in the minds of individuals here on Earth (the Greek etymology of "Utopia" suggests it is "no place"). I suspect that, were a messiah to come, she would produce no change in the majority of people and only an increased sense of shame in the remainder.

As a teacher, I encourage students to pursue questions of morality and religion. I cannot believe that the world's organized religions provide a basis for solving these questions—indeed, two millennia of horrific immorality based in theism suggest the opposite is true—but I encourage students to pose questions that matter to them, and to use evidence as the basis for answering them. Perhaps if they are especially careful about gathering and evaluating evidence, they will notice the religious foundations of much of higher education, and the ongoing search for truth that continues even at many religious institutions. One can believe in a god (or gods) and science, and although being a Christian might impede one's ability to think, it doesn't necessarily prevent it altogether. Perhaps most importantly, students will learn to protect themselves against the biases of their teachers.

With luck and perseverance, we can avoid that most unreasonable and intolerable of fates described by the long-time university administrator, Stanley Fish in the title of his January 2005 commentary in the *Chronicle of Higher Education*: "One University Under God." But it seems increasingly unlikely that we will be able to ward off religion as a replacement for high theory, race, gender, and class as the center of intellectual energy in the academy. At least religion does not masquerade as science, unlike astrology and Bayesian statistics.

There are many reasons to believe something. As I have hinted, evidence is my reason. In contrast, revelation, authority, and tradition are poor reasons to believe. These reasons form the basis for organized religion, as pointed out by the British evolutionary biologist Richard Dawkins in a letter to his ten-year-old daughter. If Dawkins can raise these issues with a ten-year-old, I see no reason we cannot raise them with our students, who are twice her age. And I see no reason to terminate our discussion of morality at the boundaries around human relationships; rather, I think we should treat non-human organisms with respect. Perhaps we should adopt the mantra of the permaculture movement: care for Earth, care for each other, share the bounty. Teaching broad-based care, and living it, is our moral imperative.

Employing skepticism is entirely consistent with using evidence as a basis for belief. I mentioned Louis Schmier's quote in an earlier letter: "Education boils down to acquiring the desire, confidence, and courage to question the answers." Imagine how much closer we would be to an informed democracy if most citizens questioned the corporations, governments, and mass media that pummel them with inappropriate messages about how to conduct their lives.

Care of Earth's millions of species is perhaps the finest example of a common good, and significant moral questions are raised by our ability and apparent willingness to exterminate non-human species. What gives us the right to destroy "God's creation" and our children's future? Are we superior to other species? How would we know? Is the survival of individual humans a greater need than the survival of entire species? How do these questions correspond to questions we once asked about races of humans? To sexes of humans? How do they correspond to questions constantly raised by society about issues of gender, identity, and sexuality?

Because evidence is the basis for scholarship in the sciences, informed argument has a long history in the academy. The final fragment of learned dispute in today's academy—the Ph.D. dissertation—provides too little indication that argument once was a proud tradition. It remains unclear to me how we managed to cast informed discourse from the academy, though I am temporarily inspired when the case for disputation is reborn, albeit briefly and with little lasting support, by the likes of Wyoming lawyer Gerry Spence and noted author Christopher Hitchens. I encourage you to promote the art of disputation with the same vigor you pursue scholarship, for both are fundamental to the acquisition of knowledge and wisdom.

In addition to encouraging reasoned disputation and questions of reason, we must restore the crumbling structure of the liberal arts in education. As Harvard biologist Edward O. Wilson writes in his poetic book *Consilience*, the ideal of unity borne of Renaissance and cultured by Enlightenment has been abandoned during the last three decades. Reform is necessary, and it must aim at the consilience of the natural sciences, social sciences, and humanities in scholarship and teaching. I agree with Wilson that every college student should be able to answer the question, "What is the relation between science and the humanities, and how is it important for human welfare?"

I think this is a vital question. But as I posed a series of questions to a Ph.D. student at his preliminary examination, attempting to build a foundation for Wilson's insightful query, one of my junior colleagues interrupted the student with his own assessment of the role of teaching in the academy: "Enough of the touchy feely bullshit. Let's cut to the chase." I assume he meant the "chase" that results in publications, preferably in his favorite scientific journal. Rude as this comment was, I suspect it merely reflected the general sentiment in the room. I fear that only the teaching-oriented student and I pondered the role of a broad education in a room full of academicians. I know I have mentioned the near absence of respect for breadth in teaching and learning among academicians, but this example should reinforce the point.

To further emphasize the point, I employ a deceptively simple assignment in each of my science courses. The assignment is designed to encourage students to answer Wilson's question, preferably in the absence of narrow-minded faculty members. I require each student to prepare a significant piece of literature or art that addresses one or more of the (scientific) topics of the class. As I described in a previous letter, students usually are hesitant, at least in the beginning, to express themselves via nontraditional means. Yet year after year, I am humbled by their efforts and proud that, when the semester concludes, they can answer Wilson's question about the relation between science and the humanities.

I encourage students to explore seemingly disparate relationships in synergistic fashion, drawing on the contributions each can make. In addition to supporting cooperative efforts on major projects, I force students to cooperate on examinations. I promised to describe this arrangement in a previous letter, and this seems an appropriate time.

After each student completes an in-class exam (with essentially no time limit), she takes the same exam again, this time with a group of three or four other students. The first three to five students to complete the exam are given a clean copy, a quiet room, and time to work on the exam together. Groups are formed continuously as students complete the exam, and each group is given a "fresh start" to complete the exam. In this way, students receive immediate feedback on the just-completed exam and they learn from each other (these lessons tend to persist longer than those that come from me). In the process, they learn to interact in a professional manner and they learn the art of argument. (Some students argue so effectively they convince their peers to change a correct answer to an incorrect one. On the second exam, students tend to focus on evidence rather than a charismatic authority figure.) A final reward—the least important, from my perspective—is an elevated grade, based on the score earned by the group: Points are added to individual exam scores based on the group exam, with an upper bound of ten extra points. This approach is difficult to implement during fifty-minute class periods, so you might need to schedule exams during evenings or replace exams of traditional length with several shorter exams.

Additional skills and concepts should be taught to every student in every class. We all need instruction in how to think and express ourselves in written and oral forms, as I have commented previously. And as I indicated in my second letter to you, we need constant reminders to live "as if" oppression did not exist, and tips about how to pursue such a life. Further, every planetary citizen should learn how to monitor his ecological impact, just as he learns how to balance a checkbook. Because the fiscal economy is rooted in the environment, it is ultimately more important to account for flows of energy and cycles of materials than to account for the dollars we spend. If you find somebody who believes the economy is more important than the environment, you should suggest he hold his breath while counting his money.

Many other important topics are to be taught. Some are general, whereas others are specific to a discipline. Again, I bring your attention to the overarching goals of environmental protection, social justice, critical thinking, and the power of expression. I encourage you to use these as guideposts as you teach. And, of course, as you live.

XIV

If your discipline is vibrant, you will be able to draw connections between it and everyday life. If it's dead, you should question why you're teaching it. You might be surprised at the breadth of topics proven by great teachers to be timely and relevant to the lives of contemporary students. These include, for example, courses in the classics and entire curricula focused on the Great Books. Never mind the undue influence of dead white men so prominent in these disciplines, much less the suggestion from some quarters that the major problem with dead white men is that we don't have more of them.

Do not be surprised to find that your colleagues and students are not as interested in discovery as you are. Rather, consider it a privilege when you find that rare individual who is interested and interesting, engaged and engaging, on the subject you hold dear. In my experience, a few students who are exceptional in this regard can be found in the honors program. Even most large, research-oriented state universities have colleges or programs dedicated to honors students. These students are worth seeking because they are more humble, open-minded, and inquisitiveness than their peers, or mine (and doubtless yours as well).

I have only recently become involved in the Honors College at my institution, and each interaction with these students and their mentors has been a breath of fresh air in the musty attic of my mind.

The students periodically drop in on my open "coffee hour" each week, during which I slake their caffeine addictions and they fill my cup with adventures of the week past. Each thinks he is getting the best deal—a free latte and muffin, a chance to mingle with his peers and me—but I know better, for they rescue me from indifferent students, disinterested colleagues, and politicians disguised as university administrators.

A greater test than these students appears in the classroom each semester: captivating the students who resist the charms of your favorite subject. This challenge provides a legitimate reason—one of the few I have found—for keeping up with the news and with popular culture. By drawing parallels between the classroom topic *du jour* and contemporary events, you could capture the interest of the most incurious student. I link the personal actions of my students to the subjects I teach; the cars they drive, the clothes they wear, and the food they eat are fair game for my courses in conservation biology and applied ecology. Individual actions have societal consequences, and I try to demonstrate how the two are connected. I fail more often than I succeed, though I have perceived some progress in recent years.

XV

If your students learn *how* to learn, they will enjoy a lifetime of learning. If they learn only *what* to learn, they will flounder shortly after they escape your reach. You must teach students how to discriminate between conflicting messages, unless yours is the last voice they hear (which seems unlikely unless you drive them to suicide). Few learned how to learn in high school. None of us know enough about it.

Small wonder, really. The entire system of public education in the United States was designed specifically to prevent students from thinking for themselves. That's a pretty strong assertion, so I will review the evidence that supports it.

In an earlier letter, I quoted Jules Henry's book, *Culture Against Man*: "School is indeed a training for later life not because it teaches the 3 Rs (more or less), but because it instills the essential cultural nightmare fear of failure, envy of success, and absurdity." Henry reached this conclusion after spending hundreds of hours in the classrooms of our public school system and reviewing a mountain of published evidence. His scathing critique of American culture strongly supports the notion that individuality and creativity are purposely eviscerated from students well before they complete high school.

The roots of the cultural crisis run much deeper than the counter-culture days of the 1960s, and well beyond the sphere of education. But education has long been fundamental to the destruction of individuality, creativity, and, for lack of a better word, soul. Consider, for example, a few words in a speech to businessmen by President Woodrow Wilson: "We want one class to have a liberal education. We want another class, a very much larger class of necessity, to forgo the privilege of a liberal education and fit themselves to perform specific difficult manual tasks." Wilson's sentiments echoed those of William Torrey Harris in his 1906 book *The Philosophy of Education*: "Ninety-nine [students] out of a hundred are automata, careful to walk in prescribed paths, careful to follow the prescribed custom. This is not an accident but the result of substantial education, which, scientifically defined, is the subsumption of the individual." In vogue with his time, Harris extended the idea of subsumption to the land as well as the individual: "The great purpose of school can be realized better in dark, airless, ugly places. . . . It is to master the physical self, to transcend the beauty of nature." As I indicated in previous correspondence, Harris was U.S. commissioner of education from 1889 to 1906.

Harris was not the only influential educator willing to express his desire for docile American citizens during 1906. That same year, the Rockefeller Education Board, a major advocate of compulsory public education, issued this statement: "In our dreams . . . people yield themselves with perfect docility to our molding hands. The present educational conventions [intellectual and character education] fade from our minds, and unhampered by tradition we work our own good will upon a grateful and responsive folk. We shall not try to make these people or any of their children into philosophers or men of learning or men of science. We have not to raise up from among them authors, educators, poets or men of letters. We shall not search for embryo great artists, painters, musicians, nor lawyers, doctors, preachers, politicians, statesmen, of whom we have ample supply. The task we set before ourselves is very simple . . . we will organize children . . . and teach them to do in a perfect way the things their fathers and mothers are doing in an imperfect way."

The statement by the Rockefeller Education Board and the book by Harris were preceded a year earlier by Elwood Cubberly's dissertation at Columbia Teachers College. The future dean of education at Stanford University wrote that schools should be factories "in which raw products, children, are to be shaped and formed into finished products . . . manufactured like nails, and the specifications for manufacturing will come from government and industry."

Tracing these ideas further back in time, we find the 1888 *Report of the Senate Committee on Education*, a summary of which is provided by a single sentence on page 1,382 of this gargantuan document: "We believe that education is one of the principal causes of discontent of late years manifesting itself among the laboring classes." According to John Taylor Gatto, award-winning educator and author of the 1992 book *Dumbing Us Down*, the committee was justifiably nervous about the high quality of education provided by nonstandardized, local schools where students were actually taught to think for themselves.

The Senate Report parallels the 1897 writings of famous philosopher and industrial educator John Dewey. Dewey's famous pedagogic creed, first published in *The School Journal*, included this thought about the role of teachers in society: "I believe that every teacher . . . should realize he is a social servant set apart for the maintenance of the proper social order and the securing of the right social growth." Cubberly provided the "proper social order" and the "right social growth" less than a decade after Dewey and the U.S. Senate supplied the rationale for herding the masses on behalf of business.

In other words, the captains of industry and leaders of government set out to create an educational system that would maintain social order (and increase their profits). How? By teaching students just enough to serve industry but not enough so they could think for themselves. Questioning the sociopolitical order and communicating articulately were not part of the plan. Americans were to become drones in a government-subsidized country ruled by corporations. While Reagan-era neo-conservatives were excoriating communism as a system in which government controls industry, they were promoting a system built upon an even worse idea, one in which industry controls government.

Mind you, the development and implementation of K–12 concentration camps is not part of some giant conspiracy. Rather, it is the outcome of the way our educational system was created. Most of the people who originally developed the system believed they were doing the right thing, and they did not try to hide their plans or intentions. It was completely consistent with the perspective, derived from religious organizations, that the domination, cohesion, and vitality of society were inversely related to individualism; permitting free inquiry and action were anathema to control by religious societies and also by corporate society. (I am not promoting excessive individualism, which begets the disintegration of law and order as it confers the "right" of an individual to disregard his responsibility to other individuals and communities.)

Today, the blueprint of "education to serve corporations" remains unchanged. Although the reasons behind the blueprint have been largely obscured by history, they are still known by many contemporary educators. As clinical psychologist Bruce Levine wrote in *Commonsense Rebellion*: "I once consulted with a teacher of an extremely bright eight-year-old boy labeled with oppositional defiant disorder. I suggested that perhaps the boy didn't have a disease, but was just bored. His teacher, a pleasant woman, agreed with me. However, she added, 'They told us at the state conference that our job is to get them ready for the work world . . . that the children have to get used to not being stimulated all the time or they will lose their jobs in the real world.'" In other words, citizens who are capable of thinking for themselves cannot properly serve the corporations that run the country.

The main point of this history lesson is simple, and you've heard me say it before: Get used to swimming upstream. Most people do not want to think for themselves (or perhaps they actually think they are doing so, which is even more terrifying). In fact, they have only rarely been asked to think for themselves. A century of standardized education in support of business pushes society ever closer to corporate hegemony and therefore, in the case of American-style capitalism, ever closer to exterminating the world's cultures and species. A fine recent example of standardization at the expense of thoughtful reflection is the federal No Child Left Behind Act, a bill strongly supported by Business Party I and Business Party II before being signed in January 2002 by the self-proclaimed "business" (and later "wartime") president, George W. Bush.

None of which gives you the right to surrender, of course. If resistance is futile, hope is lost. I beg you to join me in the fight for true education. Perhaps we can rebuild the "thinking class" of the nineteenth century.

XVI

After our many exchanges about teaching and learning, I am delighted with the question you asked in your last letter: Does the university reward teaching? I am even more pleased with your recognition that teaching offers its own rewards, regardless of the university's willingness to chip in.

The short answer, as you surmised, is "no." The modern research-oriented university rewards scholarship beyond the classroom, not within it. A solid record of scholarship practically guarantees tenure, regardless of poor teaching. Indeed, promotion and tenure committees will turn a blind eye from your teaching if your scholarship is meritorious. In contrast, evidence of stellar teaching will leave those same committees nonplussed, even critical of your scholastic record. Top-ranked liberal-arts institutions generally are much more willing to accept and reward teaching as scholarship, though they rightfully demand scholastic accomplishments beyond the classroom as well.

This discussion points straight toward higher education's mission and its reward system. In doing so, it opens the university to critical reflection and therefore to criticism. Much has been written on this subject, and I especially recommend the writings of long-time dean Stanley Fish and Harvard president Derek Bok. I possess neither the writing skills nor the intellect to do them justice by attempting to summarize their excellent ideas. Instead, I offer my own musings, centered as they are on you and your role in the enterprise of higher education.

Most institutions of higher education employ an uninspired system of "expert" journeymen, which is merely an extension of the apprenticeship your graduate education is perceived to be. Any resemblance to the medieval system is purely intentional. At the end of your journeyman period, which usually lasts six years, a jury that has already earned the title you seek evaluates your performance as a craftsman. In theory, this jury of associate professors and professors votes on your eligibility for tenure based on your life's accomplishments. In practice, the jury's decision seldom is so pure. Be that as it may, denial of tenure typically grants you a year in which to seek employment elsewhere. If the university grants you tenure, it is merely extending your First-Amendment rights to the classroom and beyond: You are now in a position, the university admits, to pursue scholastic and teaching endeavors as you see fit. Critics of higher education often perceive this admission by the university as a job for life, although nobody genuinely familiar with the process sees it that way.

As my tone probably suggests, I do not want you to think for a moment that academia is free from politics, or that academicians are capable of objectivity when making decisions about scholars and scholarship. The recognition of tenure-worthy scholars is, in my experience, influenced to no small degree by a scholar's willingness to pander to colleagues at higher rank, his views on students (in the opposite direction I would have hoped), and even his religion. I have observed brilliant tenure-track assistant professors sitting meekly at faculty meetings during important discussions, and then quickly counting the raised hands during formal votes to be sure they cast their votes only with the majority. Remember, the herd sniffs newcomers warily. More sadly, I have watched junior members of the faculty ignore their own graduate students because senior faculty members warned them about spending too much time with mere students. Perhaps most egregiously, I have seen colleagues granted tenure because their religion matched that of the powerful agenda-setters in their department even as similarly productive colleagues of the "wrong" religion were denied tenure.

Avid pursuit of scholarship is fundamentally important to the mission of higher education, and the depth and breadth of our ignorance about the natural world ensures that we will not soon exhaust meritorious topics for study. Beware, though, of the rampant confusion associated with distinguishing between inputs and outputs of scholarship. Outputs include, for example, books, papers in refereed journals, juried art exhibits, critically acclaimed music, and lasting change in the behavior of those we teach. On the other hand, generation of grant funds is an input. The typical university administrator regularly terms this "input" an "output," and rewards faculty accordingly. Indeed, earlier today, I received a thoughtless piece of correspondence congratulating the faculty for generating grant funds, as if this were a valued exercise in and of itself. I do not recall this administrator ever congratulating faculty on their scholarship; on the other hand, I'm not sure he would recognize true scholarship if it landed on his desk.

It is easy for administrators to keep track of bricks, mortar, and grant funds. Far more difficult are evaluation of scholarship and assessment learning. In addition, institutions of higher learning, which throughout history adamantly pursued and promoted scholarship even when doing so meant sacrificing materialism, recently have become a perfect reflection of society's pursuit of greed. It should be no surprise, then, that the pursuit of money often overwhelms the pursuit for truth in the academy.

Of course, not all decisions by university faculty members and administrators are motivated by finances or politics. A scant few days before my promotion and tenure dossier landed on the provost's desk, I sent him a particularly critical letter. Politically naïve, or perhaps merely unwilling to play along, I expressed my profound disgust at one of his recent decisions (the details of which seemed important at the time, though the ensuing decade has erased even the subject from my memory). As the final authority, he could have sent me packing despite positive recommendations from the departmental committee, the department chair, the college committee, the dean, and the university committee. That's why he gets the last shot, after all. But his response to my scathing letter was civil (if slippery) and he rubber-stamped his approval on my tenure dossier. I appreciated his lack of vindictiveness, if not his decision-making ability. I suspect it was the latter, and not the former, that made his tenure as provost so brief. But perhaps my cynicism is getting the best of me.

Letters to a Young Academic

I could not have been more excited to initiate my career in my current department when I was hired more than sixteen years ago. Not yet thirty, I possessed barely a hint of cynicism and my optimism was not unlike yours of today. The preponderance of gray heads in my department, and the hope that I could help replace them when the impending wave of retirements began, were primary reasons for my excitement. Who wouldn't relish the opportunity to select their own colleagues? And what better way to build strong and positive relations with my peers than working with them to select our future associates? I suspect that many departments offer the opportunity to build relationships with current peers while selecting future ones. But not all do. In particular, I call your attention to the last bastions of top-down administration, the land grant colleges of agriculture. I hope you'll see a rise of faculty governance in these colleges, which typically has been paid only lip service until now, during your career. I'm not hopeful, though, based on my own experience.

As I had expected when I was hired, I have served on several faculty search committees during these last sixteen years in a land-grant college. But, in an unexpected turn, I now dread this duty. Indeed, I shun every opportunity to provide any form of input into faculty searches. This is no simple case of cynicism, however. In my department, mean-spirited and dishonest faculty members have turned searches into grudge matches and raw displays of power. Thanks to deceitful faculty and poor communication by the department head, faculty searches are divisive games of tit for tat, and numerous former colleagues refuse to speak to each other. The process by which we recruit new faculty members is a veritable "how-to" guide. Actually, it's a "how-not-to" guide. Allow me a lengthy explanation, which simultaneously allows me to vent steam and perhaps allows you to walk into the storm with a full set of raingear. Perhaps you'll choose to stay indoors, though I commend that step to you as a last resort, as it has become for me.

In my department, each search begins with a job description written by one or two people hand-picked by the department head. The position description invariably bears a strong resemblance to its author(s). Given that the author(s) rarely seek substantive input from other faculty, this is no great surprise. The department head then names the author(s) as chair(s) of the committee before hand-selecting the remaining handful of committee members. For the latter, the typical approach is to choose one member from each of the three traditional disciplines in our large and disparate department, and then he tosses in a graduate student advised by one of the search committee chairs. In the usual case, the committee is comprised of about a half-dozen members, including two co-chairs and a graduate student closely allied to one of them.

Even before the application deadline, the faculty stands divided. The department has not vetted the process by which faculty will be hired, and there are no stated rules. Most members of the faculty have not been given an opportunity to influence the process or even discuss it. Some are not yet aware that we are filling an opening. Obviously, this undemocratic (perhaps even antidemocratic) "process" is a prescription for mounting suspicion and plummeting morale. The department head never reveals how or why he selected members of the search committee, and the committee chair(s) are not asked to defend the position description. The faculty does not discuss, much less vote on, the position description because most of them are not aware that a search is under way.

I could suggest myriad recommendations here, but they should be relatively obvious. They have to do with democratic principles of faculty governance and transparency on the part of administrators. I've mentioned all of them to my department head, to no avail. According to Edward Abbey, society is like a stew: unstirred too long, the scum rises to the top. Apparently I've not been stirring with sufficient frequency in my department (or society at large, for that matter).

A recent example demonstrates that the situation can spiral downward from this point, and illustrates how poor administration can undermine faculty morale and departmental productivity.

In one particular case, the search committee was evenly split, with a small group of "disciplinary" representatives, including me, and a similarly small group of co-chairs and their graduate students. Along with the other representatives in the former group, I felt fortunate to have some influence over the hiring process, though I had no idea why I was selected. I pleaded with the committee co-chairs and the department head for a faculty meeting to discuss how we should conduct the search, and I begged for a faculty vote on the candidate to whom we would offer a job. Both requests fell on deaf ears.

Initial meetings of the committee were surprisingly productive, and we unanimously settled on the top two candidates within a couple of amicable meetings. The department head had given us permission and funds to conduct three interviews, but we were split about the third-best candidate, so we decided to interview only two. With respect to selection of a third interviewee, I recall that half the committee preferred one candidate, a couple members preferred another, and one committee member preferred a third. Importantly, this final candidate's lone voice of support came from one of the committee co-chairs. When the committee broke up from our second meeting, we left the committee co-chairs in charge of reporting to the department head and arranging the two interviews.

Imagine the committee's surprise when the first candidate scheduled for an interview was not among the top two candidates. Or even the top four. Rather, the meeting between one search committee co-chair and the department head produced an interview for the candidate who was supported only by the search committee co-chair.

Enraged, I approached the department head and the co-chair of the search committee. Each pointed the finger at the other, the department head claiming that my colleague had told him the initial interviewee was among the top three and the search committee co-chair claiming that he'd been overruled. I will never know who lied; perhaps both did, which would come as no particular surprise. Not long before, the search committee co-chair had been a colleague: We had co-taught courses, co-advised students and employees, and co-authored successful grant proposals and journal articles. I can no longer bring myself to work with him, and we barely say "hello" when we pass in the hall. Incidents such as this one, which are all too common in our hallowed halls, let the snakes into the proverbial snake pits of academia.

One bad event often leads to another, and an evenly—and contentiously—divided search committee left the final decision in the hands of the department head, who took full advantage. An opportunity for faculty input was promised, but it culminated in a vote only to the extent that not stating adamant opposition to a candidate can be considered a vote. Nobody was particularly surprised when the department head chose the candidate rated so poorly by the search committee. Perhaps he was justified in doing so, though the fact that she had no teaching experience and no refereed publications must have weighed on his mind. In sharp contrast, the other two candidates we interviewed had respectable and well-documented records in teaching and research; one was already internationally acclaimed for his scholarly contributions to the literature, and he had received rave reviews based on two years in the classroom.

In addition to her poor record of scholarship, our newest faculty member was poorly matched to the department's needs. She was not well qualified to teach the classes she was expected (and hired) to teach, and her research was not complementary to the department's mission. She hung on for a few years, wrote a couple of papers based on her dissertation research, and fled for another university at the first opportunity. She couldn't be happier. But, through no fault of hers, she left a badly divided faculty in her wake.

In the years since our new colleague sought and found greener pastures, several departmental faculty joined her in the exit lane, and several others began shopping for jobs. The number of faculty in the department has reached an all-time low because the department head cannot seem to garner the dean's support to fill vacant positions. If I were the dean, I wouldn't approve any positions requested by our department head, either, because he has a terminal case of ineptitude (or so it seems to me and many of my colleagues). The dwindling number of faculty who remain here do so for personal reasons or because they lack the credentials to flee. My credentials are very strong and I'm fairly certain I could go elsewhere. But I've spent many years sinking deep roots in my neighborhood and I have strong familial motivation to stay.

Despite a strong desire to stay, I spent a year quietly looking for a job elsewhere. I did not relish the thought of uprooting my family and leaving our home, but I was afraid the dean would put our department on the chopping block when the state legislature sent the next round of expected draconian budget cuts in our direction. For that matter, I still fear elimination of the department, if only because I would rather flee for a location of my choosing than for one forced by hurried desperation. But my abbreviated quest for employment elsewhere let me know I am very particular about where I will live, and extremely reluctant to leave the students I've come to know here.

Even though it appears I will be staying here, I am no longer excited about the prospect of choosing my colleagues. Recent experience indicates that even my colleagues can lose my trust, and my department head's reluctance to give up decision-making authority to the faculty makes it easy to think about departments with democratic tendencies.

There is a short moral to this long story: Beware the politics of division. This way of life is popular at the national level, and it is accelerating the disintegration of the American Empire (which is not necessarily undesirable, especially for cultures and species other than our own). But such politics need not consume your fledgling career, thereby pitting you against your colleagues. Any energy you are willing to invest in development of a collegial community of scholars is worth the alternatives of division and despair, and I certainly wish I had spent more time salvaging the frayed relationships before they became tattered and torn beyond hope.

There is a more immediately pragmatic reason to avoid the politics of division: You never know when a colleague will be asked to give an opinion about you. The co-chair of that long-ago search committee is in a position to offer his opinion to search committees at other institutions, and I've no doubt he will when the opportunity presents itself, thereby interfering with my ability to migrate elsewhere. This minor inconvenience illustrates that the sea of academia is surprisingly small, viciously turbulent, and filled with predators. On most days, the sea is tinted green with envy and is filled with ruthless competitors because the stakes, minuscule though they are, still are slightly larger than the individuals chasing them.

I implore you to hold onto threadbare relationships with colleagues as long as you can. But do not sacrifice yourself in the process of saving your department. You can lead a perfectly productive career working with colleagues outside your department, and this approach could save your sanity and the morale of you and the colleagues you choose to keep at arm's length. Better to appear aloof than engaged, if the engagement is inevitably hostile.

XVII

Institutions of higher education are largely self-governed. Individual faculty members, even those in state-funded colleges and universities, lie beyond the grasp of legislators, if only because elected politicians and their appointed counterparts lack the attention spans to interfere with the day-to-day operations of the university. You can make your institution a better place to work by taking up the task of committee assignments.

Potential stumbling blocks are ever present, however. First, committees reflect society in being comprised almost exclusively of individuals incapable of acting rationally. See, for example, the overview of Jonathan Singer's *The Splendid Feast of Reason* in my third letter to you. If you belong to the small minority of people Jonathan Singer terms "rationalists," the pace and often the direction of committee affairs will frustrate you. Second, the political motivations of most committee members will add to the frustration. And finally, the contentious nature of academicians, especially with regard to departmental affairs, often makes committee service a thankless and painful task.

Youthful exuberance once made me believe that all academicians were committed to the life of the mind, and were able to set aside differences in politics, worldview, and the common quest for parking on behalf of the pursuit of knowledge. Now I realize that the corner office and the premier parking space are more important to many academicians than truth or justice. Perhaps, as is often pointed out, we are driven to pettiness and jealousy because the academic stakes are just that small.

Although my own experiences at helping run the academy have proven less than fulfilling, I nonetheless encourage you to partake. Your interpersonal skills far exceed mine, which suggests that your patience and tolerance could help you facilitate institutional change in ways that my own impatience and intolerance have not. On the other hand, if helping administer your institution produces returns consistent with mine, you might want to turn to the more rewarding arena of professional societies and the general citizenry.

Professional societies put a public face on your discipline. How can you contribute to these societies while ensuring your own success? The options are varied and diverse, including holding an office, chairing the annual meeting, editing the newsletter, and thousands of others. I have been particularly inspired by service on review panels for agencies and organizations that distribute funds to peers and (especially) students. Serving on these panels serves society while broadening my horizons. They allow me to interact with interested, interesting scholars. Serving as a panelist for various governmental agencies and nonprofit organizations provides glimpses into worlds I would not imagine otherwise, giving me fresh perspectives and allowing me to learn. They are more focused and intense than professional conferences, and usually more rewarding.

I have greatly reduced my participation in professional conferences during the last decade, be-

Letters to a Young Academic

cause I prefer to use my limited research funds to send my students to conferences instead of attending them myself. They need the trip more than I do, and, if I've chosen them wisely and supported their efforts appropriately, they've earned the trip with their intellectual (and occasionally physical) sacrifices. Furthermore, my disgust at the typical conference seems to increase with my participation in them. A recent conference dedicated to sustainability provides an excellent example: The conference "break" food was imported from thousands of miles distant, we met in a conference center that served as a paragon of American imperialism, and the conference website prominently featured livestock production (an inherently unsustainable enterprise). In short, the conference's fuzzy signal was obscured by the noise of the meat-eating, aquifer-depleting, SUV-driving, cell phone-using conference organizers. With misbehaved "friends" like these, sustainability needs no enemies. With only slightly more effort, the meeting organizers could have provided positive examples by holding the meeting in a more appropriate facility, serving locally grown fruits and vegetables, and encouraging or providing public transportation for meeting participants.

On the other hand, I will be the first to register when I seen an advertisement for the conference of my dreams. This conference focuses on the collapse of industrial "civilization." Such a collapse would wreak havoc on my 403(c), my 501(k), and my IRA. But it might save a few of the species and cultures that have managed to elude our iron fist, and that's worth much more than the few dollars in my retirement funds.

If your scholarship is relevant to society—which, as you doubtless realize by now is a characteristic I admire—society might seek your advice. Some of my most rewarding experiences have resulted from interactions engendered by my scholarship. Colleagues from government agencies and nonprofit organizations periodically seek my advice about protection of natural resources. Occasionally, they solicit a letter or report that criticizes environmental destruction or (less frequently) praises constructive activities. I am pleased to respond to these requests, not because they always help (they seldom do), but because they provide much-needed encouragement for the very few hard-working individuals who spend inordinate energy swimming upstream against the mighty current of resource-consuming, planet-destroying, spirit-crushing neo-conservatives currently in power.

This is more rewarding than you can possibly imagine, though I hope one day you will experience the thrill yourself.

XVIII

The signature line on your recent letter—"Little Brown Mouse"—suggests an unwarranted crisis of confidence. If you insist on berating yourself on the basis of your accomplishments, please allow a little objectivity into the analysis. I understand and even appreciate, albeit in a sick, twisted, and highly personal way, your sentiments as you compare yourself to faculty who have been doing this gig far longer than yourself. But that doesn't mean I can just let you continue to bask in your inferiority, albeit perceived only by you.

And it doesn't mean that I won't continue to compare myself to scholars both more accomplished and more senior than myself, in a strident quest for self-humiliation that drives over-achievement. Never has Jules Henry's "fear of failure, envy of success" been so evident as in the day-to-day life of overachieving academicians. Yes, I'm calling you an overachiever.

In typical administrative style, I counted the number of invitations we had each received at your stage of career. These are invitations to deliver seminars, participate in workshops, speak in symposia, or author papers (including book chapters, journal articles, and so on). And they include all such invitations: local, regional, national, international. This is a flawed statistic, as any single metric would be, but it does provide a reasonable single indicator of the fame you have achieved thus far. The *curriculum vitae* you sent earlier this year indicates you had garnered fourteen invitations by about six months ago. For myself, at your career stage, the number was four.

It appears that your level of productivity, hence fame, is not nearly as pathetic as you'd like to believe. Buck up, little brown mouse. You're the academic equivalent of a rock star.

Sincerely,

Mid-Sized Gray Mouse with Torn Ear and Chewed-Off Tail

XIX

Theoretically, your institution and profession value you in direct relation to your ability to supply scholarly contributions and to make the contributions known. There is no reason to value yourself on the basis of these two metrics, but also there is little harm in acknowledging how the academic game is played and then adhering to a few of the less dreadful rules. It never has been clear to me which criterion is the more important of the two, though the former necessarily precedes the latter. Beyond some nebulous minimum standard, however, it is apparent that the ability to create the perception of scholarly productivity is more important to university administrators and distant colleagues than productivity itself. This is consistent with the oft-expressed idea that quantity is valued to a greater extent than quality, which occasionally is articulated as, "my dean can count, but he can't read." This is a shining example of the old expression: In theory, there is no difference between theory and practice, but in practice, there is. It accounts, at least partially, for the production of Least Publishable Units in refereed journals.

Bricks and mortar, the lines on the resume, and especially the grant funds you generate are easily counted and highly valued by bean-counting administrators. In contrast, generation of meaningful scholarship, creation of a scholastic community, and cultivation of lasting change in individuals and societies are challenging undertakings that are notably difficult to document. In the words of Albert Einstein: "Not all that is counted counts, and not all that counts can be counted." I encourage you to keep working on the things that count in the hope that someday those things will be counted.

In addition to pursuing and documenting scholarship that matters to the lives of individuals and the conduct of societies, you should be able to describe your scholarly contributions in language that is readily understood by other scholars, the general public, and even university administrators. As an example, you should be able (if not necessarily willing) to create a 200-word press release that publicizes each piece of scholarship. This is no small feat, and it will require patience and diligence on your part.

Promoting your own scholarship verges on self-aggrandizement, and you should take care to deflect any hint of glory toward colleagues, co-workers, and administrators. If we are to help create a just, sustainable society, we must focus on the ideas, and not their intellectual source: "Look at the moon, not the finger," as the Buddha said. (I know I've used this line before. I just can't seem to help sharing pithy Buddhist quotes.)

Wendell Berry cogently comments on the propensity of many academicians for shameless self-promotion, and suggests that we are not far behind doctors and lawyers in this dishonorable endeavor. I encourage you to avoid the pursuit of individual fame at the expense of the common good; as with teaching, your scholarship should be marked by humility. (This is one of the few points with which I agree with Berry's shockingly misinformed antiscience screed, *Life is a Miracle*. At the outset of this tiresome bit of spiritual poetry, Berry informs us that he is not a scientist. Then he boldly proceeds to misinterpret and misrepresent the point, process, and outcomes of science.)

Establishing a holistic, integrated program of scholarship is different from, and, in my opinion, superior to, hopping superficially from topic to topic. The former provides an opportunity to engage multiple scholars at various levels of understanding while adding richness and depth to a substantive topic. Peeling away multiple layers of misunderstanding or ignorance in pursuit of core knowledge can be deeply rewarding. In addition, colleagues and administrators often reward such obsessive pursuit, if only because it keeps you from infringing on their scholastic turf.

I have little advice regarding your program of scholarship, and have therefore spent few words on this topic in my previous letters. There are two reasons for my brevity on this matter: (1) You have already established your ability to conduct excellent scholarship en route to the terminal degree in your field, and (2) based on your personal and professional history, I have no doubt you will continue to excel in this arena.

Your accomplishments clearly exceed mine at a similar career stage, as I indicated in my previous letter. As a result, I have little basis on which to question your scholastic pursuits or products. I have no doubt you will continue to excel if you keep doing what you've been doing for these past few years: letting your curiosity lead you along the path of knowledge and discovery, keeping track of the discipline's forest while documenting the structure and function of the individual trees—and even the branches, in some cases—and, in short, loving and respecting your life's work. That your enthusiasm for the subject carries over to the classes you teach and the service you conduct is further evidence of your passion. In my experience, this passion provides its own reward. An additional reward is evidenced by the numerous scholars of teaching and learning who indicate that great teachers are great scholars, that great teaching is fired in the oven of scholarship. Mind you, my view of "scholarship" is much broader than the narrow definition typically recognized by academe: Great scholars integrate and synthesize without necessarily generating the "products" held dear by large, research universities.

Outstanding teachers keep track of the important intellectual developments within their fields, conduct research or practice their art, develop original thoughts on their subjects, study carefully the activities of others in their fields, and take a strong interest in the broad issues of their disciplines, from history to epistemology. In short, they perform the intellectual, physical, emotional, and artistic work they expect of their students. Great teaching is unlikely to emerge from poor scholarship.

As you hone your detective-like skills in pursuit of knowledge and understanding, I recommend you start thinking about your first sabbatical leave. You likely are eligible *upon* promotion instead of the following year (the latter being when most academicians begin to ponder the sabbatical leave). If I am correct, I would recommend you file a sabbatical proposal coincident with your promotion materials, the approval of which is contingent upon your earning tenure. It will take a little time to nail down the logistics for your sabbatical application (such as letters of support), especially if you intend to spend some time beyond your current metropolitan area. I further recommend taking a full year's leave, versus the portion taken by many. You will spend a month or two at the beginning and end of the sabbatical leave dealing with cumbersome logistical details instead of thinking deeply, and it seems impractical to make these few months a significant fraction of your time away (much less a majority). The reduction in salary will be rewarded richly by the additional time to contemplate and experience a "new" version of life.

A final, albeit minor recommendation for your sabbatical leave (and perhaps beyond it), regards the telephone. Even when silent, it lurks as a threat to your thoughtful reflection. When you are riding the wave of reflection or scholarship, unplug it. The world can get along without you for a little while. And don't even get me started about cell phones.

XX

You might be the best academician in history, but you aren't the first. You'll be even better if you take advantage of the knowledge of your predecessors. They can alert you to scholastic goldmines and political landmines. They love to bask in your reflected glory, so they'll provide great advice for nothing except a quickly mumbled word of thanks. And they can teach you a thing or two about becoming a mentor yourself. Few lessons have been more valuable to me than the wisdom of my mentors; my goal—my passion, really, for it is what causes me to literally shake with excitement when I rise each morning—is to become a worthy mentor for you and your successors.

Mentoring has its roots in Ancient Greece. When Odysseus went to war, he placed his son in the care of a trusted friend named Mentor. Mentor was as a protector, teacher, and guide for Odysseus's young son. Academia is neither war nor, for most academicians, an escape from war. But given the many pitfalls to success in academia, you can benefit greatly from a mentor.

The pragmatic reasons for seeking counsel from your mentors are many and varied. Any reasonably observant academician who has been in the department for a few years has learned many lessons from their years of teaching and service on committees. They know how to create an effective agenda, push (or pull) decisions through appropriate channels (and, when necessary, inappropriate ones), and find out who has power. The good ones can influence a meeting's outcome before it even begins by strategically planting rumors, changing the venue, and misdirecting key background information. In the March 2004 words of Ms. Mentor, the *Chronicle of Higher Education*'s advice columnist, "They know how to be Gandhi or Genghis Khan, as needed."

I encourage you to seek and use many mentors: Any number can play, and each of them will appreciate the opportunity to influence the career of a rising star such as yourself. Any decent academician is a raconteur at heart, so your mentors will revel in the stories of their past as only someone present at that long-ago scene is capable. After a few tellings of any given story, they'll be thankful for your audience and even more thankful for the absence of witnesses to correct factual errors that unerringly arise with the passage of time.

In addition to teller of tales, mentors should assume many roles. An individual mentor could be a teacher, showing you how to fix the jammed photocopy machine, prepare an application for sabbatical leave, or avoid confrontations with the department's surly silverbacks. She could be an archive of historical information about departmental policies and politics. She could be an adviser, a reliable listener and dispenser of thoughtful counsel. She could be a guide who knows when to lead, when to follow, and when to get out of your way. If she is good, she will recognize that this is *your* journey, not hers, and will therefore nudge, cajole, assist, or avoid you in much the way Virgil guided Dante on his journey (there will be times you'll wonder why

Dante's travels were so pleasant and carefree). Thus, mentors are teachers, advisers, guides, coaches, critics, and constant sources of intellectual stimulation and honest feedback. Each mentor should be, in some way, a role model. Some of my best mentors were those who clearly illustrated how I should *not* act, and you will be wise to absorb this knowledge as well as the grace and tact of your more polished mentors.

It is not necessary that your mentors become your friends, but it is imperative that they place your best interests above their own. This is no small sacrifice in a culture that encourages backstabbing competition at the expense of cooperative altruism. If you find mentors willing to help you, hang onto them and return the favor to future generations of academicians.

Lest I give the wrong impression, your mentors need not be old hands to know the departmental ropes or otherwise offer sage advice. Early-career members of the faculty often are more attentive to the literatures of pedagogy and your scholastic field than older colleagues, and they often are more willing to attempt new techniques in and out of the classroom. Youthful enthusiasm often enables them to see connections between disparate enterprises, which could make them adept teachers, colleagues, and grant-writers. They are less likely than older professors to have forgotten what you're going through, and therefore are likely to be sympathetic to your station in life. Those who have recently gone through the tenure and promotion process might offer particularly insightful advice as you prepare forms, statements, and your psyche.

As you develop your mentoring skills, which already are excellent, I encourage you to give all you can to those who would call you "mentor." Give them articles and books about scholarship and pedagogy. Given them free rein to make choices and take risks. But give them advice if they stray dangerously. Better yet, provide this advice in advance. Freely give them your time. By giving them yourself and expecting nothing in return, you open the door to a world of pleasant surprises. If your experience resembles mine, you will be repaid many times in installments large and small.

As he neared death, one of my early mentors scheduled his funeral and provided plenty of advance notice so that I, along with his other protégés, could help carry him out of this world. Most of us don't plan our lives with the precision and thoughtfulness with which he planned his death. Few of us have that choice, of course, and some might view it as a bit macabre. But it's difficult to find fault with his attention to detail in the face of adversity.

I launch this paper boat with a final bit of advice about the life of the mind: Never take it for granted, for it could be snatched away tomorrow. The life of an academician is challenging, to be sure. It demands stamina of the mind and occasionally of the body. It requires personal sacrifice for the common good, a profession and life on full public display, and a predisposition to swim upstream against a strong cultural current. It is not for the faint of heart or the feeble of mind.

But the rewards are supreme. You are allowed to live a life of leisure, in the historical sense: You choose the work you do. Through the lives of your students, you experience life and death and the wonderful emotional roller coaster of youth. As such, you can choose to remain forever young, if only vicariously. You have opportunities to serve as a mentor. And, if you are worthy and fortunate, somebody might endow you with that noblest of distinctions by calling you "teacher."

About the Author

Guy R. McPherson is an award-winning teacher and researcher at the University of Arizona. He has taught courses at Grinnell College, University of California-Berkeley, Texas A & M University, and Texas Tech University, and has delivered guest lectures and seminars at numerous other institutions. His published works include dozens of scholarly articles and five previous books: *Killing the Natives: Has the American Dream Become a Nightmare?*, *Applied Ecology and Natural Resource Management*, *Changing Precipitation Regimes and Terrestrial Ecosystems*, *Ecology and Management of North American Savannas*, and *Glossary of Fire Management Terms Used in the United States*.

Professor McPherson advises and mentors undergraduate and graduate students in several disciplines. In addition to his academic experience, he helped develop and administer The Nature Conservancy's David H. Smith postdoctoral fellowship program in conservation biology.

www.ingramcontent.com/pod-product-compliance
Ingram Content Group UK Ltd.
Pitfield, Milton Keynes, MK11 3LW, UK
UKHW020147180426
470027UK00014B/67